THIS IS IT!

Fanfare . . . puh-*leease*! Sound the trumpets! Bang the drums! Here it is . . . the ultimate guide to the most favorite games in all of Nintendo®-game-land—the guide your letters have all been demanding—the guide to the most successful (indeed, LEGENDARY) Nintendo games ever to appear on your home video screen—the SUPER MARIO BROS. games!

Jeff Rovin, the author of *How to Win at Nintendo Games I, II* and *III*—not to mention *How to Win at Nintendo Sports Games*—is back again with what is possibly his greatest Nintendo games book of all! While making sure that none of the mystery or enjoyment is taken away from the SUPER MARIO BROS. games, he gives you in-depth tips and analysis of each succeeding level of SUPER MARIO BROS. 1, 2, *and* 3—as well as providing you with a special section on how to be your best at *Super Mario Land*!

Quite simply, this is a book no SUPER MARIO BROS. games lover worth his or her salt would want to do without. The indescribably entertaining worlds of the SUPER MARIO BROS. games will never seem quite the same!

HOW TO
WIN
AT
SUPER
MARIO BROS.
GAMES

Jeff Rovin

ST. MARTIN'S PAPERBACKS

How to Win at Super Mario Bros. Games is an unofficial guid
not endorsed by Nintendo®.

Nintendo is a registered trademark of Nintendo of America In
Super Mario Bros., Super Mario Bros. 2, Super Mario Bros.
Super Mario Land and Game Boy are all trademarks of Ni
tendo of America, Inc.

HOW TO WIN AT SUPER MARIO BROS. GAMES

Copyright © 1990 by Jeff Rovin.

ISBN: 0-312-92449-6

Printed in the United States of America

St. Martin's Paperbacks edition/December 1990

10 9 8 7 6 5 4 3 2 1

CONTENTS

INTRODUCTION

Mario!

Videogame star and TV star—named, it is said, after an employee at Nintendo's U.S. headquarters—his image is on notebooks, stickers, cereal boxes, comic books—you name it.

Who'd have thought such fame awaited the feisty little carpenter when he made his videogame debut back in 1981? Then, he was the more or less anonymous nemesis of the charismatic monkey villain Donkey Kong in the Nintendo arcade (or "coin-op") game of the same name. In fact, Mario even became something of a bad guy in the arcade sequel, *Donkey Kong Jr.*, in which the player took the part of the big ape's offspring as he tried to rescue Pop from Mario's cage.

Things really began to cook for Mario when he was given his own game, *Mario Brothers*, in which he and his brother Luigi—making his videogame debut—had to clean crabs, turtles, and other vermin from a sewer system. *Mario Brothers* was po[ular] enough to spawn a sequel, *Super Mar[io] Brothers*, which was really a creative and comme[r]cial breakthrough: the game designers placed M[a]rio in a fantasy land where there were opportuniti[es] to create imaginative foes, landscapes, power-up[s] and a wonderfully complex quest. The game was [a] smash, and when Nintendo made the move in[to] home videogames in 1985, *Super Mario Brothe[rs]* was the first cartridge produced for the new Ni[n]tendo Entertainment System.

The unassuming "Everyman" hero proved wild[ly] popular, and sequels followed. Each of the four M[a]rio adventures has been different, with new se[t]tings and foes—yet each game has maintained t[he] fundamentally nonviolent charm and boundle[ss] sense of wonder that made the first Mario game [so] popular.

Where will it end?

It's too early to say whether Mario will join t[he] pantheon of great media heroes like James Bo[nd] and Donald Duck, whose immortality is assured.

But he's getting there.

And speaking of *getting* somewhere—

We hope this book will help *you* get somewher[e,] namely, to the end of Mario's many journey[s.] Within these pages you'll find never-before-reveal[ed] tips and details about the games, as well as t[he] first-ever, in-depth coverage of 1990's super-hit, S[u]per Mario Bros. 3.

So—Wart are you waiting for?

Let the games begin!

SUPER MARIO LAND

bjective:

In all the world, there was no more contented realm than Sarasaland. Then, one day, a black cloud loomed overhead and the alien monster Tatanga emerged, conquering Sarasaland by hypnotizing its inhabitants. Adding insult to injury, Tatanga decided to wed Sarasaland's Princess Daisy. Enter Mario, who vows to cross the four kingdoms of Sarasaland—Birabuto (World One), Muda (Two), Easton (Three), and Chai (World Four), each of which consists of three lesser realms—to rescue Daisy before the nuptial day, defeat Tatanga, and liberate Sarasaland.

ameplay:

Many lethal creatures work for Tatanga, and to defeat them, Mario must leap and land on top of them *or* butt them off the Blocks on which they're stand-

ing. Along the way, he obtains various power-u
items. Each Heart you nab gives you an addition
Mario; one hundred Coins also provides an extr
Mario. (Note: most Blocks give one Coin. Som
noted below, give more—how many Coins you g
from these depends entirely on *how fast you repec*
edly strike the Block). You can also get Stars, Flo
ers, and Super Mushrooms. Super Mushroom
increase Mario's size—that is, cause him to becom
"powered-up" as Super Mario—Flowers enable hi
to throw Super Balls at foes. (Only one Super Ba
can be on the screen at a time; one Ball kills *bot*
parts of two-section creatures like Nokobons an
Mekabons; but, sadly, some creatures, like Hone
are impervious to them.) Stars make him invincib
for short periods. You'll know when your invinc
bility is about to run out. A theme from *Orpheus*
the Underworld plays through twice. When it end
so does your imperviousness. Be advised, howeve
that you're invincible *only* when it comes to en
mies: if you fall off a Ledge, you'll die. These iten
are all located inside ? Blocks. Blocks from whi
Super Mushrooms emerge when Mario is not Sup
Mario will give forth Flowers when he is. If yc
can't get these items immediately, don't panic. U
less they fall into water or off a Ledge, they rema
onscreen for as long as you're in that screen. Mar
also has a submarine, Marine Pop, and an airplan
Sky Pop. These are used only in Worlds 2/3 ar
4/3, respectively. When you fire their guns, no mo
than three unexploded projectiles can appear on tl
screen at once.

Another power Mario possesses is manifested primarily in treasure rooms. In addition to collecting Coins, you'll be breaking Blocks in the walkways for points and power-ups; this will leave holes in the floor. (In some rooms, the Coins are already hanging over gaps in the walkway.) How, then, do you get across the gaps? Simply keep the B button pressed down. That will enable you, literally, to walk on air! This skill also works at the beginning of 2/2.

If Mario dies at any point in the game, you don't lose any of the Coins or points you've amassed, though your next Mario starts back a short distance in most cases. In a few sections of the game, he actually starts *ahead* of where he died! The Nokobon platform at the end of 2/2 is a rare example of that.) And while any foes you've killed will usually remain expired—the Honen at the start of 2/1 are an exception—the new Mario can get all the ?'s again. Likewise, any foe that may have been about to attack when you entered a Pipe, will be gone when you emerge. By the same token, before you enter any Pipe, be certain you collect any Coins or power-ups from ? Blocks to the immediate right of the Pipe. The ? will be replenished when you emerge, allowing you to "double-dip."

Finally, just in case you lose track of the time, the music will speed up when you have just 100 seconds left.

Points:

These range from 100 for each little squirt that at
tacks, to 5000 for the bosses of each level ... and
Tatanga. A Super (that is, "powered-up") Mario also
earns 50 points for shattering Blocks; normal Ma
rio can't shatter them. (Note: creatures that can de
tach body parts grant more points when killed in
one piece than if each section is slain separately.
Just make sure you *do* kill both parts, however, as
the remaining part may regenerate what you de
stroyed.) Points are also awarded for each Coin col
lected. In every level, you're playing against time,
so don't dawdle!

Strategies:

Each of Sarasaland's worlds is divided into three
sections. Here's how to get through them all.

1/1: There's a Coin in the first Block, a power-up in
the second, and a Coin in the third. Get on the third
Pipe and press down: there's a Coin room inside.
Upon emerging, collect a Coin from the Block
above. (As noted above, in situations like this,
you get the Coin *before* going into the Pipe, you can
hit the Block and collect again when you emerge.)
Stop at the foot of the plateau ahead. There's a Chi
bibo on it, so stand there until the little fellow
comes down, then jump on it. When you reach the
first row of Blocks, either hurry to the right before
the two Chibibos drop from the Ledge, or stay to
the left until they emerge from under the row.

you're underneath, the Blocks will prevent you from jumping and stomping the creatures, and you'll perish. (Unless, of course, you've shattered the Blocks and can jump up in the narrow channel. However, it's a tricky move and not worth the risk.)

After dispensing with the twerps, get the Coin in the ? above. Beyond the next Pipe is a row of six Blocks. Hop on them, go to the right, then jump down and get the Coins as you fall. If you miss them, get on the ?, smash all the Blocks on the upper left, leap back onto the Pipe—assuming you haven't scrolled it too far left—and try again. (If you fail at this, wait till you get Super Ball power across the Pit and shoot left to nail the Coins.) When you're underneath the row, collect the Coin from the lonely ?, then jump onto that Block and hit the row above: the second Block from right contains a 1-Up. Jump onto the row of three Blocks to the right, hop up and hit the ? on top, then leap onto it and get the power-up. (If you're Super Mario, make sure that you don't inadvertently smash the Blocks below the ? before you use them as stepping-stones! Otherwise, you won't be able to get the power-up.)

A Nokobon comes next; jump on it then get away *fast*, or its Bomb will explode. Obtain a Coin from the ? after the Pipe, at which point you'll arrive at three rows of Blocks. None on bottom can be broken, so don't bother trying. Just hop onto the second row, collect Coins from all the top Blocks, drop back down to the bottom row, then butt all the Blocks in the second row for Coins. Leap the Pit:

the Pipe there takes you to a Coin room. (Remem
ber: first get the Coin in the ? to the right.) If you're
a non–Super Mario, bounce off the ceiling as you
go along the bottom tier—that is, press the control
ler right and keep jabbing the A button repeat
edly—this will save a lot of time. When you leave
the room, there are Coins in the next two ? Blocks
As soon as the second ? appears, a Fly will com
after you. Flies hop, then rest for several seconds
jump on top of them immediately after they hop
Next up is a Pipe to the left of a stack of Blocks
Jump onto the Pipe, using a Super Ball on the Ch
bibo down there—or jump down on it if you don'
have Super Ball power—then hop onto the stack
Wait there, and shoot the Chibibo when it ap
proaches. Now jump, hit the ?, and grab Star whe
it floats down. (If you'd hit the ? *before* blasting th
second Chibibo, the Star would have drifted dow
right on top of it. Where would you be then?) Invi
cible, you can race ahead.

The next row of Blocks is all Coins. If you misse
catching the Star, watch out, again, that you don
get trapped underneath as a Chibibo enters fro
the right. The next two ?'s have Coins. Your invi
cibility should carry you through the first Fly tha
attacks . . . and, if you hurry, the second as well.
not, kill them as before. (Regarding the first Fly:
you've run out of invincibility, you can stand ato
the Pipe. When the Fly jumps up at you, it wi
usually self-destruct.) Get the ? (a Coin).

The Sphinx on the other side of the Pit can't hu
you, so just hop over. Above it you'll find a row

which the last (unmarked) Block contains many Coins; you can get up to 15 if you strike *fast*. Just keep butting the Block until it's empty. At the pyramid-like structure made of Blocks, get the lower row of Coins first. (If you get the upper row first, the screen will scroll to the left so far that you may not be able to get back down to them.) If you're Super Mario and thus oversized, simply stand on the first Block on the left of the lowest Coin row—*not* the Block jutting to the left, below it—squat, and fire a Super Ball at the Coins. The Ball will collect them for you! Go up to the second row and squat *squarely* on the Block at the beginning of the second tier of Coins. Fire a Super Ball to collect the Coins. If you have trouble with that, you can always try for the second row by getting behind the Pyramid, leaping down—which you'll do to collect the string of Coins floating there—and shooting to the left at the Coins.

Upon reaching the Tower at the end of the level, use the Elevators to get into the door at top. (Note: you can stand directly underneath the Elevators at the end of many levels and jump *up* onto them, instead of leaping from the sides. The advantage to this is that you can position yourself so that you'll be at the very edge of the Elevator when you leap on, already facing toward the right. If you have to waste time positioning yourself *after* you're on the Elevator, your fine-tuning may cause you to miss your ideal jump-off time.) Entering the Tower on top, you'll access a bonus stage: there, you must press the A button as if the controller were a slot

machine. If your timing is right, you'll win a goo
many extra lives! If you enter the Tower's bottom
door, you get diddly! Because of that fact, if tim
threatens to run out when you're near the very en
of a level, it's better to *let* it do so than to compr
mise and go in the bottom. At worst, you'll gai
back the life you lost by going in the top door. A
best, you'll add two lives to your storehouse of Ma
rios—three, minus the one you sacrificed.

1/2: When you come to the first three Blocks, ge
the ? last if you're not Super Mario; inside is
power-up which you'll have to chase as it falls t
the level below. While you're on the next platform
be aware that the Chibibo isn't bound to its pla
form to the right; it can come down and get yor
Your next foes will be a pair of Bunbuns: Spea
dropping Flies. You can leap on top of these to ki
them, or you can simply wait until each drops
Spear and then dash under it. There's plenty of tim
to do so. The next ? is a Coin, after which you'
cross five platforms. (Watch it—there's a pair of N
kobons here, so hit them with Super Balls or pour
on them and scurry before their Bombs go off.)

After dispatching a Chibibo, you'll reach a ro
of Blocks with a Coin in the center—and a Nokobo
on top; butt the Block and it'll fall off. Look dow
to the right, and you'll see a ?. Jump down . . . b
shift Mario so that he lands to the *left* of this. The
carefully, move to the far left of the platform—dor
move *too* far left, though, or you'll drop off the side
and leap up. There's an Invisible Block here. Hit

and you'll release a 1-Up. Catch it, get the Coin from the ?, then jump up on the ? Block to get to the platform to the right. There are a pair of Elevators: when you leap from the Elevator on the right, do so when it's quite high; that way, you can gather the loose change hanging in the air on your way down.

More Bunbuns attack moments later: two in the air, a third high in the air, a fourth flying very low. You can jump on the first, second, and fourth; to kill the third, rebound a Super Ball off the ground. At the Pyramid, watch for the two Chibibos coming down, then climb to the top and get the ?, a power-up. (You'll have to scoot to the right, to the lowest Ledge on that side, to catch it. Just make sure you don't scoot *off* the edge of the Pyramid!) There's a trio of Elevators to the right: take them fast and you'll be in good position to get the Coins to the right; that is, a rapid crossing will place you on the third Elevator while it's high. Immediately go to the far right of the Ledge you're on, so that you're standing just under the Ledge with the Nokobon (don't worry: the Bomb-toting Turtle won't come down at you). Another Bunbun will attack, but you'll be safe from its Spears here. When the flying fiend leaves, jump up, either killing or avoiding the Nokobon. The next row of Blocks contains a Coin, a 1-Up, and a Coin, in that order. There's a Coin in the ? below, but no Invisible Block this time.

At the next Elevator—there's just one this time— jump to the right in such a way that you can gather the three horizontal Coins on your way to Ledge.

Two Bunbuns attack in tandem; stand as if the la
tree on the right were passing through you, a
their shafts won't touch you. Fire to the *right*
each one is leaving: your projectile will ricochet
the left and kill them. When you reach the fin
Elevator, just before the Tower, once again go f
the top door and the bonus stage. There are tw
Blocks hanging in the air to the right of the E
vator, and you must use these as stepping-stones
get into the Tower. Thing is, you've got to get
and off them super fast: they fall apart in less th
a second. You won't die if you drop, but you wo
be able to get into the top door. Don't lose heart
one of the fragile Blocks falls: you can still get
with just a single Block. The trick is to stand
the very edge of the Elevator and jump as soon
it's lined up with the word "Battery" on the l
side of the Game Boy.

1/3: Whatever you do on this level, don't lose yo
power-up ability. Much of the treasure here
quires Block-bashing ability. To begin with, go *le*
so that you're standing just to the right of the w
there! Jump up, and you'll uncover a secret Ele
tor above your head! When you do so, clear out t
Coins from the ?'s on the right—taking care not
scroll the Elevator off the left side—then go back
the Block on the left side of the row, get on top
it, jump left to the Elevator, and ride it to a sec
cache of Coins—28 beauties in all! You'll miss
on the wonderful things below, like Falling Ro

and Pakkun Flowers, but try not to be disappointed!

When you reach the edge of the upper Ledge, look down. Wait until the Pakkun Flower retreats into the Pipe below you, then jump in. (This Pakkun stays down for a long time, so there's no need to hurry.) Once inside, go to the middle level, smash the Blocks above, go down, break the Blocks below that, then drop to the floor and bust up the Blocks there. You'll get the points *and* be able to cross the gaps and collect the Coins by pressing down the B button. Note: the second breakable Block from the right, on the bottom, contains many Coins. Just keep hitting it!

Leap the Pit when you emerge, and you'll come to four Pipes. The first two don't contain Pakkuns, but the second two do. Get on the second Pipe, wait until the Pakkun Flower goes down on the third, leap onto it, then vault over the fourth Pipe entirely. There are Coins in the row of ? Blocks you'll encounter overhead, but watch out: stop under the first ? on the left and then *immediately* back away to the left. Falling Rocks will drop just beyond that. Stand still till they stop, then get the Coins. There are more Coins in the next row of Blocks overhead, but they won't be as easy to get since a Gao is guarding them. If you have Super Balls, run ahead, stand beneath the left torch, just to the right of it; fire, run back to the left. The Ball will ricochet and eventually hit the Gao. If you *don't* have Super Balls, wait until the monster fires, then hurry onto the row of Blocks and jump down on the creature.

Watch out, though: Gao can shoot up as well
down, so don't think you're immune just becau
you're above the creature! In either case, crack t
Blocks and bop the ?'s when the menace is end
When you're finished, go *back* to the empty spa
where you destroyed the Block on the right—t
space to the left of the ? on the far right. Hit
again, at the empty space. Another secret Eleva
will appear! Hop on, and it will lift you to a Pi
the top of which has a very well-stocked Coin roo
After collecting the Coins on the bottom, break t
Blocks immediately overhead and gather 24 Coi
in there. To reach the ones on top, you'll need
fire a Super Ball. Climb on the exit Pipe to get t
foursome above it, then leave.

There's nothing in the small Pyramid that 1
lows. When you get over it, hop onto the lowest ti
which contains Coins. If you're Super Mario, ju
up, shattering the Blocks ahead, and get the Co
from the ?'s. (Don't worry: the Nokobon can't le
its Ledge.) When that's done, hop up and use a
per Ball against the Turtle, then get the Coins
that tier. If you have the time, press down on 1
controller so that Mario is squatting, then press
repeatedly so he can shimmy down the tunnel, (
lecting Coins. If you are running out of time, j
stay on the Ledge where you killed the Nokob
go right, leap over the wall, turn, squat and fir
Super Ball left down the middle walkway to coll
the Coins. Stand. Jump into the right angle form
by the Blocks above you—the vertex is in the up
left corner—and an Invisible Block will appear.

t repeatedly for Coins. Head right, over the Pyramid, after pausing to make sure the Falling Blocks
here have already fallen!

Now, then—remember, above, where we said, "If
ou're Super Mario . . ."? If you're *not*, all is not
st! Instead of busting the wall, fighting the No-
obon, and so forth, just squat and go right along
he lowest passageway. This gives you access to the
yramid laden with Coins. Just don't go rushing
n, though: those Falling Rocks mentioned in the
ast paragraph will welcome you as you enter the
reasure chamber! There's also a power-up in here.
Vhen you reach the other side of the Pyramid,
hatter the Blocks to get out. You'll come to a pair
f Sphinxes beneath a double row of Blocks: smash
hem all and acquire a power-up. Leap the Bridge
hat lies just beyond it, or you'll plunge to oblivion.

As soon as you get to the other side, stop: a Gao
s lurking on the far right, spitting fireballs, though
hey can't get you if you stand where you are. Just
ait until it's fired one, then charge! You'll be able
 pounce on it before it gets off another shot. Im-
nediately after fighting one more Gao, you'll face
ing Totomesu, the boss of the level. It'll take five
uper Balls to kill him; straddle the fourth and fifth
locks from the left, leap his first fireball, and shoot
n the way down. If you have no Super Balls, you
ust leap over the creature; as soon as the music
hanges, run to the right as fast as you can. Jump
s first fireball, then run under its second. There's
 brief interval before the next two-fireball se-
uence: run *right up to its nose* and jump over the

boss . . . making sure, when you do, that you cl
the creature's tail. You're trying to land in
small space behind it, not on the monster its
(And don't try to kill the beast by landing on
head, as you can do with lesser Gaos—you'll d
Once you leap the monster, it'll explode. (Anot
option: if you're Super Mario but have no Su
Balls, you can run right *through* the monster. Yo
lose your power-up, but if time is running out, i
a viable choice!) Step up to the stone barrier beh
the creature, and the wall will come down. Yo
enter a chamber where Daisy will appear . . .
only to tantalize you! She'll turn into a Fly a
vanish after a moment, and you'll have to proce
to—

2/1: There are Coins in the ?'s in the first row
Blocks. After that, jump down along the right v
of the plateau on which you're standing. Not
where the Honen is leaping from the water, th
stand on top of that spot. It will perish when it
the bottom of your feet. Hop up two plateaus a
dispatch the next Honen in this fashion, collect
Coins above, then hop back to the left, down
plateaus. Now jump onto the bottom plateau to
right and stand on the left side. Jump up and yo
uncover an Invisible Block with a power-up. L
onto the Block and pluck the Flower. If it's a Su
Mushroom, you can't catch it while standing a
where on that Ledge; you're going to have to na
while leaping to the Ledge to the right. Otherw
it'll fall in the water.

Continue to the right. After crossing the two Elevators, get the power-up from the ? to the right of the Pipe, shoot Super Balls to get the Coins to the right, then drop down the Pipe. Once inside, step onto the platform on the floor, just to your right. Hit the uppermost block, which is *attached to the wall to your immediate right.* You'll get a power-up. Don't pluck it ... yet. Go to the left of the platform, hop onto the row of two Blocks and, from there, jump up onto the single Block above. Leap up and smash the Block that leads into the upper cache. (Note: if you accidentally break one of the stepping-stones while leaping up, that's not good .. but it isn't necessarily disastrous if you have Super Ball power. Crack the Block that leads to the upstairs section anyway, go to the bottom section, and we'll tell you what to do in a moment.) Jump up and collect all but the rightmost row of Coins up here. Go to the wall on the right, carefully snatching or Super Balling the top two Coins—leaving the two below it untouched—then leave this area. Obliterate all the breakable Blocks on the left side, then go to the bottom section and gather the Coins there. When you're finished, get on top of the exit Pipe, leap up to obtain the two remaining Coins, and leave. If you were unable to get into the Coin room above, *don't* leave until you've turned left on top of the exit Pipe, squatted, and fired a Super Ball. It will ricochet into the room and clean out all but one or two of the Coins.

Outside, you'll collect Coins on several plateaus, then come to a series of Bridges with Coins along

the top. You can avoid the Honen using a stop-a
go technique, or you can watch where they emer
and stand on top of them as before, killing the
when they pop up. At the end of the first Brid
wait until the Nokobon comes along on the secon
Jump up and Super Ball it. If you don't have Sup
Ball power, wait until it turns and is headed rig
before proceeding. If you leap on it and kill it ri
away, you may run into a Honen leaping right
side it while fleeing the Turtle's Bomb.

As you continue ahead, deal with the Honen
described above. Keep an eye out for the pair
Chibibos that arrive in tandem. If you jump on
first, be sure you jump again *immediately* on
second, or it'll run into you and kill you. Don't si
ply leap ahead to avoid them. Even though they
wander to the left and drop off the Ledge like lit
lemmings, you may jump right into the Honen
ing and falling on the right! In the row of Blocks
the right, you'll find a Coin in the left and a S
in the right. You'll have to leap to the right to ca
the latter as it emerges. Be careful: a Chibibo
wandered onto the plateau below, so make sure y
land on its head as you fall.

Run quickly while you're invincible, and yo
be able to get past the fire-breathing Yurarin: i
attack right after the fourth plateau beyond
floating Coins. This creature turns to fire at y
once you pass, so don't pause to take a breath j
because you got around it! (Whether you caught
Star or not, it's a good idea to make the Pipe y
goal; as soon as you've made it by the Yurarin, ta

a big leap over the Pipe and press yourself against the Pipe's right side. The Yurarin's fireball won't get you there.)

The next Pipe is another Coin room. Before entering, go to the ? on the top right: multiple Coins can be found here. When you do enter the Pipe, you might be inclined to panic: after clearing the Coins off the floor, you'll notice that there doesn't seem to be any way out! Fear not. Go to the bottom right corner and jump up. This will reveal an Invisible Block which will enable you to leap up to the Coins *and* get out. Use the B button technique described earlier to cross the gaps in the walkways. However, on the lower walkway, stop before you reach the last gap or you *will* fall through it. You won't perish, but you'll waste time getting back up there. Note that you can smash the Blocks directly below the Pipe exit above.

Upon emerging, again use repeated hits to get the Coins from the ? Block above, gather the floating Coins to the right, and pluck a Coin and power-up from the left and right, respectively, of the row of Blocks above. Immediately after this row, you'll face a Yurarin. Jump its fireballs and position yourself on the Bridge so that the killer will come up under your feet and die. If you don't, you've got a problem: a second Yurarin pops up to the right, and if the other one is still on your left, you'll be caught in a dangerous crossfire. If this happens, leap their fireballs while edging to the right. (Do this even if you've killed the first Yurarin ... though facing one is obviously a whole lot easier!)

Wait until it's fired, then run to the right and jum
over it, onto the Ledge to the left of the Elevato
If you time your jump right, you'll have the unpa
alleled satisfaction of actually grazing the Yura
in's head on your way over, killing it . . . a ne
bonus.) Once the Yurarin is off the screen, it'll n
longer fire at you. Get on the Elevator, stand o
the left side, and as the Elevator is rising, bust th
Block and the ? Block above: in it is a 1-Up. You
have to break them both *and* jump to the Co
Ledge on the right before the Elevator descend
the 1-Up falls onto the Ledge and keeps rolling;
you don't get to the Ledge immediately, the 1-U
will fall away. Get the 1-Up and Coins both, the
leap onto the top of the wall to the right and ta
a hefty jump onto the Elevator. (Note: if you're n
Super Mario, you can't get the 1-Up because yo
can't break the Block underneath it. Sorry.) Mal
a quick leap onto the platform by the Tower do
and enter on top.

2/2: Your first foe here is a Mekabon, which o
taches its Head and sends it soaring down at yo
Luckily, it isn't a homing head. As soon as you sta
the round, rush right, get on the Ledge, and jur
on the Head before it comes off. If you fail at th
you can attack the Head and body separately
simply stay out the Head's way. When it reattach
itself to the body, leap up and come down on top
it. So long Mekabon. Use the B button to run acro
the string of Blocks and gaps to the right. Ther
a power-up in the first Block; it'll drift to the righ

and you'll have to jump to catch it. Make sure that when you do, you land on top of the wall *or* on the Chibibo waiting for you. You'll find a Coin in the second ?. Before you can crawl down the Pipe, it will be necessary to kill the Nokobon on top. Jump onto the Block to the left of the Pipe, and either fire at or hop on the Turtle to kill it. If you did the latter, quickly leap back to the Block on the left or onto either side of the platform on which the Pipe is resting, to avoid the Bomb. When it detonates, get on the Pipe, hop up to grab the Coins above, then drop down.

In the Pipe, the uppermost Block on the wall immediately to your right contains multiple Coins. As you did in the 2/1 treasure room of this design, take care not to shatter any Blocks. Follow the same procedure here as you did there. Leaving the Pipe, get the Coin in the ? to the left (again), then collect the Coins above and head right. There's a Coin in the next two ?'s, and then a pair of Elevators; climb onto the ? you last hit to board the horizontal transports. However, be alert: when you leap off the second (last) Elevator, jump high so you can sweep up the vertical line of Coins to the right. As you fall, shift to the left so you land on the Pipe and not on the Nokobon to its right. If you land on the creature, get onto the Pipe *fast* or you'll blow up!

If you're not Super Mario and you don't want to face the robot to the right, just hop to the stone Ledge on the right, then step off to the left; an invisible walkway extends slightly over the water. Proceed on the lower level. Harvest all the Coins

here, facing only minimal opposition from a trio o
Chibibos. Deal with these by staying to the left sid
of any tunnel in which they appear, just to the lef
of the column: that's the only area where there'
room enough for you to jump. Wait for them to re
turn to the left before making a leap onto their no
gins. (Note: if you choose to go across the top, stan
on the Ledge to the upper right of the Pipe, wa:
until the Mekabon's head reattaches, then leap u
and attack it. Up here, you won't get nearly a
many Coins, but you *will* find a Star in the la
Block on the right of the first overhead row. Cros
on top, kill the Mekabon below you at the othe
end, then jump down and get the Star.) Your rel:
tively safe passage ends when you come to a N
kobon waiting for you on the other side. Wait unt:
it starts walking right before you jump over. A Ch
bibo will attack; leap on it, then kill the Nokobo
and dodge the fireballs of one of your old friends,
Yurarin, who's rising and falling on the right. U
ing the Blocks on the ground to shield you from t!
flame-spitter, leap when the monster goes dow:
timing the jump to hit its head when he rises: ot!
erwise, you'll have it breathing flame at your ba
while you deal with the Mekabon that arrives o
the right.

After crowning the robot—head and body bot!
remember, or it'll regenerate—you'll come to a pa
of Elevators, the first one moving vertically, t!
second horizontally. When you reach the row
Blocks with a single Block above it, hit them all f
Coins. Mind you, the Nokobon and Yurarin to t!

right may have something to say about that: so, when you leave the Elevator, jump onto the Ledge as the Nokobon is walking to the right. Walk with it. When it turns left, you turn left as well: when you clear the leftmost ?, jump up, land on the Turtle, then run to the right under the row of ?'s to avoid the blast. Clear out the ?'s, then, between fireballs from the Yurarin, climb up and get the Coin from the ? on top. Jump down onto the big Block to the right—the fireballs can't touch you here—then time your jump to kill the Yurarin as you leap to the Block on the right. If you fail at this, hurry and get behind the Block to the right of the Pipe, where you'll be safe. Kill the Chibibo below you, get the Coin from the ?, then wait until the Pakkun Flower in the Pipe to the right sinks away. When it does, hop on, get the Coins above, and slide into the Pipe. Clean the Coins from the bottom, then stand just to the left of the leftmost Block of the second row. Jump up to uncover the Invisible Block here, and ascend. Make sure you don't leave before butting the left Block under the exit Pipe: there are multiple Coins here.

Exit, get the Coin in the ? to the left, grab the Coins above, and hop on the Blocks to go right. Hit the ? for a Coin, then climb onto that Block and try and hop to the Elevator which shifts from side to side. (Miracles happen!) This leads to the top door. More than likely, you'll have to take the Block staircase. Be *real* quick about it: each Block collapses the instant you step on it! There is no bonus stage at the end of this round.

2/3: This level is all water and it scrolls *by itself* you just go along with the flow. Stay mostly towar the left of the screen, darting ahead to sweep u the Coins, then getting back. If you're Super Mari look for existing gaps in walls; that's less you' have to shoot in order to fit through. Blast Yurarii the *instant* they appear: their fireballs are deadl even underwater. Torion will not only come at yc from the right, they'll turn if you haven't shot the and come at you again from the left (though on once). Don't shoot or touch the Gunions: they won bother you if you don't bother them. Touch ther and you die; hit them with projectiles, and they spl in two and attack. Also, if you get to the left of Block and you get scrolled into the left side of th screen, you'll perish.

Pay attention to your surroundings, there a items to collect: a power-up in the first collection Blocks on top, and, perhaps most importantly, Star in the second set of Blocks on the bottom. Ju make sure you're quick once you uncover it. Bein so close to the bottom of the water, the Star is swa lowed up quickly by the sands. When you obta invincibility, hurry to the far right, shooting ahea (Remember: you're impervious as long as the so runs!) When the last bars of music sound, return the left. Upon reaching the first Column which h a narrow channel in the bottom, blast the low four Blocks to get a power-up. You can really ra up the Coins when you come to the region whe they spell MARIO—just sweep up and down on th left; no enemy will bother you here. And blast just below the midsection of the Column ahead for a Heart. (If you want a big advantage here, do something to kill yourself after you get the 1-Up. You'll come back to life *before* the MARIO Coin section, and will be able to add as many lives as you want to your collection!) Watch for the last (fourth) Column in this series of Columns: the top section contains a power-up. Note: on this level, if you're Mario and you run up against a wall of Blocks, you need only clear out one tier to get through. Super Mario requires two. That *can* be a handicap if you're busy fending off fish. Note: any projectiles fired by creatures, such as Yurarin, do *not* disintegrate when the monster dies. Keep an eye on these while you're battling the source! These can be especially dangerous while you're passing through channels in the Blocks: if they enter the other side while you're inside, you're cooked!

You'll be battling Tamao and Dragonzamasu at the end of this realm. Tamao is a blob that cannot be destroyed. Thus, all you can do is avoid it. While so doing, you must also fire at its boss, behind it. Dragonzamasu spits fireballs that have to be dodged while you shoot at the creature. It takes 20 hits to destroy Dragonzamasu . . . though, fortunately, it isn't necessary to slay it. When Dragonzamasu rises, get behind the Block in front of it—you can use this Block for protection from the boss's fire when he's down; it can't hit you here, though Tamao can. Shoot the three Blocks of the bottom row to the right. Dart into the narrow tunnel you've

created. When Dragonzamasu rises again, slide
the left and rise slightly, knock out the three Block
on the row above it, and pilot your ship on into th
opening to win the round

3/1: When the Batadon arrives—which it does, i
stantly—shift to the left. It will fly in that directio
at which point you must run to the right, jump
the Pipe, get the Coin, and leap over the Pit . . . a
before the Batadon flies right. There's a Nokobo
at the second Pipe, but that won't present a pro
lem. There are two rows of Blocks, and a power-u
in the rightmost Block on the top. Get it, then lea
quickly across the Bridge that follows, since it wi
collapse beneath you. Land on the Nokobon on th
other side, then watch out when leaping onto th
Pipe to get the Coin in the Block on the right:
Cannon that fires Gira is in the next Pipe to th
right. You can step on the projectile to stop it .
but, frankly, it's less risky to avoid it altogethe
Just time your progress so that you can get on t
of the Cannon Pipe when the Cannon is submerge
(Note: you can stand on a Pipe when the Cann
comes up, and rise on top of it. You can also sta
to one side or the other on the Pipe and not be hu
when a Gira is launched. What you *can't* do is t
to get up while the Cannon is firing!) Slip down th
Pipe, getting the Coins by leaping over the Spik
carefully.

When you emerge, get to the ? on the top rig
there are multiple Coins in here. Unfortunately,
Batadon guards it. When the creature is to t

right—and this strategy goes for all the Batadons
you'll face on this level—leap onto the Z-shaped
Ledge to the left, above you. (You can't hide under
that Ledge: it'll get you there, even though it looks
as though the creature can't fit!) Step on the Batadon's head when it comes after you. (Note: if the
Batadon kills you, take heart in the fact that it
won't be there when you go to your next Mario.)
You can get up to 17 Coins from the Block above!
You'll have to kill the Nokobon to the Ledge on the
right in order to get to the Elevators. Upon reaching them, note that the middle one is extremely
narrow, so don't jump with your usual abandon.
You'll find a Pakkun Flower in the next Pipe, and
a Nokobon on the Column to its right. This is tricky:
if you don't have Super Balls, you must to hop from
the Elevator onto the Turtle, then *immediately*
jump onto the Column to its right *or* back to the
Pipe—if the Pakkun is submerged—to avoid the ex-
plosion. In either case, leap onto the Turtle *only*
when it's on the left side of the Column, or you'll
perish. Use Super Balls, if you have them, to reap
the Coins floating between the Columns as you
jump overhead.

After the Columns, you'll find a Pakkun Flower
in the first Pipe and a Cannon in the second. Hop
over the first, wait until the Cannon goes down,
then jump onto the Cannon Pipe and continue on
your way, making sure you collect the Coins from
the Blocks overhead. Be prepared to face your first
Tokotoko; the wonderfully animated stone head
runs at you, rattling its fist. You can stop it by

jumping onto its Head or simply leaping it and l
ting it run past. A second Tokotoko will drop do
at you from the Ledge to the left of the verti
Column of floating Coins. As soon as it does so, a
other Batadon will attack. Bop the Tokotoko befc
the winged creature arrives, then deal with it
you did the first one you faced—the landscape
virtually identical. Collect the Column of Coi
then climb the Blocks to the right, drop down, a
jump up to get a Coin from the ?. You'll be standi
on another Z-shaped Ledge. Climb down to t
Ledge on the right, jump up, and you'll uncover
Invisible Block with a Heart. You'll have to le
the Pit to the right to catch it ... and, when y
do, it's important that you drop down through t
gap to the Ledge below as *fast as possible*, sinc
very dogged Batadon will show up within momer
Go back to the Z-shaped Ledge and kill it as y
did before. (Here's an alternate plan you can t
before hitting the Invisible Block, step onto
Ledge to the right of the Z-shaped Ledge and go
the right edge. That'll bring on the Batadon. Ca
fully walk back to the left and *step* up onto the
shaped Ledge. Don't jump back up onto that Led
or you'll bump into the Invisible Block and unco
the Heart; with the Batadon there, you'll never
able to get it. Kill the Batadon as before, and tl
uncover the Heart.)

Upon the creature's demise, climb to the rig
stomp the Nokobon, collect the floating Coins in
vertical Column, then jump down onto the ve
cally shifting Elevator. Transfer to the horizoi

one, mindful of the fact that there's a Cannon in the Pipe beyond, and one in the Pipe beyond that . . . so you'll have two of them firing at you while you're still on the Elevator! Leap onto the Giras as they pass, to destroy them, or simply hop over them, then jump on the first Pipe when the Cannon goes down. Hit the Block above for a power-up, then leap onto the second Pipe when the Cannon's down, and *be on your toes*! Jump off and *rush* ahead to the Ledge beyond, the one on which the Pipe is sitting—it's a row of Blocks comprised of ?'s. A trio of Tokotokos comes rushing along, only *these* Heads turn once they reach the left side of the screen and attack again! If you're on the left side of the Ledge, you can jump down and bop them. If you're *really* good, you can actually graze the Heads of at least two of the Tokotokos as you leap onto the Ledge, killing them. Once the running Heads are defeated, leap immediately onto the Coin Ledge to the left, so that you can be above the Batadon when it arrives. You'll be able to leap down on it, then go under the Pipe Ledge, bash the ?'s, and collect the Coins. Take care not to get hit by the Cannon in the *next* Pipe, and also keep an eye out for the two Batadons and more Tokotokos which attack.

Surviving these, you face an even tougher challenge: Ganchan riding. The Ganchan are boulders that come rolling at you from the right. They'll kill you if you let them . . . but they're also your ticket over the Spike fields that follow. (Note: the instructions refer to the Spikes as "Needles." Sorry, but somebody needs glasses! Those deadly shafts are fat

and tapered; something must have gotten lost
the translation from Japanese.) Go to the edge
the Block wall where the Spike fields begin. Sta
facing right, with Mario's foot *over* the edge of t
wall, on thin air. When the rock comes along,
will go under your foot, pick you up, and carry y
through the air. As soon as you reach a wall
Blocks, however, make sure you get off or you
perish. (If you fall on Spikes as Super Mario, h
off quickly and you'll survive.) Position yourself
that wall as you did on the previous one, with
foot over the side, and hitch a ride on the next Ga
chan. Repeat until you come to a Ledge shaped li
an inverted L in the air. Get on the left (lower) si
of the Ledge, and wait until the Ganchan has co
down. If you stand on the right side, this rock wo
give you a lift—it'll kill you! As soon as the boul
has rolled down at the Ledge, leap to the right,
top of the object. Ride it to the wall and get off
fore it sinks down into a Pit. Leap the Spikes to
fat, horizontal Ledge laden with Coins. Wh
you've cleared these away, leap onto one of t
Ganchan which will materialize on the upper rig
Ride it to the Elevator, and hop from this into
top of the Tower. If you missed that Coin Led
don't worry, you can proceed along the bottom. J
hop from the small outcrops, over the Spikes, to
Tower at the end. These leaps are relatively e
to make, provided you start *at once*. Those G
chans that materialize at the right begin bounci
in your direction. Nor do they disappear. They
keep rolling left and right where you have to ju

making your passage difficult, to say the least! However: let *one* appear. Allow it to roll after you until you reach the Tower. Then: hop on top of it, ride it to the Elevator, and leap up into the bonus room.

3/2: In the early going, the most dangerous foe you'll face are the Suu: spiders that resemble the Stalactites in which they hide, making them tough to spot while you're looking out for other foes! Still, they're easy enough to avoid if spotted: if you inch forward, you'll trigger the arachnid's descent. All you need do, then, is quickly back up a bit, wait until the Suu goes up again—as Hemingway said, "The Suu Always Rises"—then rush ahead.

The first Suu falls after the third Pipe. (There's nothing in these Pipes, so don't bother checking.) After you pass it, you'll face a Nokobon. Bop it and clear the ?'s overhead: all contain Coins. There's another Suu and Nokobon ahead—easily dealt with—followed by a Pipe with a pair of Suus beyond it. "Trigger" the Suu on the left by getting onto the Pipe and dropping down to its right—but not *so* far right that you're under the Suu! When the spider on the left has started up, run ahead; you'll clear the second Suu before it drops. (If you want to kill them, wait until they're down and then jump on their backs.) There's a Pakkun Flower in the next Pipe: when the plant retreats, get on the Pipe and stand there until the Suu beyond it has come down. Leap onto the Block in the Waterfall, and from there onto the Coin Ledge. Sweep up the money

and stop on the right side of the Ledge: a differe
kind of spider, a Kumo, makes its debut here, ho
ping along like the Flies of 1/1. As soon as it's b
low the Ledge, fall onto its back, killing t
creature.

Hop onto the Column to the right to trigger t
Suu, then proceed to the next Coin Ledge .
watching out for the Suu overhead. Get below t
Ledge and hit the last Block on the right for
power-up. Continuing to the right, you'll find a Co
in the Block overhead. Cross the Waterfall by ho
ping the Blocks, then *quickly* dispose of the Nok
bon on the Ledge. A Kumo will arrive almost
once, and if you have to deal with it and the N
kobon, you'll have your hands (and feet) full. Th
Kumo will attack you on the Ledge where you'
standing, so be ready to leap up and land on top
it. When you've killed the beasts and cleared aw
the Coins, get beneath the Ledge. Break the Bloc
as you did back in 1/3 to reveal a hidden Elevato
Ride it to the top and jump *left*—using the A butto
don't try walking on air with the B button or you
fall. Enter the Pipe and collect the 100 Coi
therein. There's also a power-up in the ?, which y
may need to break Blocks in this treasure roo
when you leave the Pipe, gather the Coins to t
left, then drop off the Ledge.

When you continue to the right, it'll be necessa
to leap onto a thin Column. If that weren't difficu
enough, you have to get off it *immediately*: a S
lactite will fall, killing you if you linger more th
a moment. (When you jump onto the Column, ma

sure that the Nokobon on the Ledge beyond is
headed to the right. Otherwise, you'll hop onto the
Column and then to the Ledge, where you'll land
on the Bomb-bearing sucker!) After killing the Nokobon, you'll have to get past a pair of Suu. Wait
until the first one comes down, then leap on its
back. You can't wait until it rises and then jump:
the arc of your leap will carry you right into the
creature's furry legs. Run over the second Suu as
well, kill the Nokobon on the Ledge, wait there for
the Kumo to arrive, jump on it, then leap to the
right, clear the Coins from the Ledge, cross the Waterfall, and get the power-up from the single overhead Block ... watching out for the Gira being
launched by the Cannon in the Pipe to the right.
Hop the Cannon—or get on top of it and then leap
to the other side—and hug the right side of the Pipe:
there's a Suu overhead, waiting to drop. When it
retreats, clear the Coins from the Blocks overhead.

After crossing the Waterfall, you'll encounter a
Kumo on the first Ledge. Be on your guard so you
land on it! (Incidentally, you'll find with this and
most previous Kumos that if you position yourself
beneath the 10's numeral of your Coin counter,
you'll be in an ideal position to jump onto the creature.) Cross the other Ledges (no problem!) and
you'll find yourself at a Spike Pit—keep an eye out
for a Block with multiple Coins here. Ride the Ganchan across ... only on this level, you have to leap
onto the boulder to get aboard. To time your leap
right, wait until the rock has hit the Spikes and
has just begun its ascent toward the left before

jumping. Get off, leap onto the next Ganchan
cross another Spike Pit, then watch out: there's
world of trouble awaiting you on the other side
You'll face a Cannon in the next Pipe, a Kumo o
the other side, and a Suu above. But all is not a
bleak as it seems: when you leave the rock, hug th
left side of the Pipe. Get on top of the Cannon—tha
will trigger the Suu—leap the ugly arachnid whe
it descends (and when the Kumo is on the right
then crush the Kumo when you come down. A sna
If you opt to go down that Pipe, you'll find a mu
tiple Coin Block near the center of the treasur
room. Also: if you don't want to go Spike hoppin
you can access the lower row of Coins by getting
them from below. Even if you're not Super Mari
you can hit these Blocks and get the bottom row
Coins. Ride the Elevators to the right—taking ca
not to die when bopping the Nokobon on the Ledg
between them, *and* making sure you jump from th
left Elevator when it's low or you'll expire whe
you hit the Stalactites above—and you'll come
those same fragile Blocks you've had to deal wit
at the end of the last few levels . . . except that
you fail to cross *these*, you won't just lose out on th
top room of a Tower. You'll perish! The trick he
is *not* to step on each one. There are two Block
then a solid Ledge, then another two Blocks. Lea
on the second one from the left, quickly hop to th
solid Ledge, then jump *not* onto the next Block b
onto the one beyond it. Leap off at once. If any
the Blocks after this one collapse before you can g
off them, you'll land on solid ground below, whi

leads directly to the Tower. You won't get to the top room . . . but you won't perish, either!

3/3: After you pass a Pipe and two Columns, you're going to face five tricky Elevators: the first, third, and fifth slide from side to side; the second and fourth shift diagonally to the upper right and left, respectively. To cross: when you reach the first Column, do *not* jump at once onto the first Elevator. Wait until it comes back a second time. In quick succession, go from it to the second to the third, then stop. Wait until the fourth comes near, then go to it and then onto the last one rapidly. When you hop from the last one, watch out: a Ganchan comes rolling along. Jump over it. Collect the Coins from atop the Pipe, cross a Column, and get onto the Elevator. Do *not* jump onto the Column to the right. Rather, ride the Elevator up and jump quickly onto and off the collapsible Blocks and over to the Pipe. Just make sure you time your move so that you land on the Pipe when the Pakkun Flower is down. Inside is a power-up and 100 Coins.

Upon leaving the Pipe, hop onto the second Column to the right and jump up: there's an Invisible Block with a power-up here. Get onto the rightmost Column and leap onto the Kumo. Get back on the little wall to the left; another Kumo will arrive. Stand there and simply drop down on it. Go to the ledge above to collect not jut the Coins, but a 1-Up in the fourth Block from the right. Six Elevators await: the first moves from side to side, the second to the upper right, the third to the upper left, the

fourth vertically, and the fifth and sixth horiz[o]
tally. You can actually avoid the sixth if you wi[sh]
but there are Coins you can only access from th[e]
Elevator—and every one is precious at this lev[el]
Immediately after the Elevators is a Pipe. Th[ere]
are Coins, as well as multiple Coins in the bott[om]
Block on the center. Just be careful not to fall [in]
the Spikes!

When you emerge, you can reach the Ledg[e]
above by uncovering an Invisible Block to the ri[ght]
of the Pipe. Hop the Ledges to the next Pipe, wh[ere]
it will be necessary to board the horizontal Ele[va]
tor below. Make certain that you do so while [it's]
moving to the right, or you'll die. Hop up from [the]
Elevator when it passes below and to the right [of]
the Ledge overhead. Jump from that Ledge to [the]
top Ledge on the right, then down onto the Eleva[tor]
when it's shifting to the right. Jump from the E[le]
vator to the Ledge on the right, then up to [the]
Ledge on the left, then to the top Ledge. Fall a[nd]
go right. When you reach the "altar" of Blocks [a]
Batadon will arrive: leap onto the altar when [the]
flying monster goes left, then jump down onto it[.]
Tokotoko is waiting on the other side, but wo[n't]
present much difficulty. Vault onto the next alt[ar]
get a power-up from the leftmost ? and Coins fr[om]
the two on the right. Just don't get flattened by [a]
Ganchan, which comes rolling down from the st[air]
on the right. Leap the Pit and clear the Coins fr[om]
the next row—this time, watching out for a Ba[ta]
don. All you have to do is get on top of the ? [box]
and jump down on the monster, then clear out [of]

Coins. Climb the next set of steps and leap the Waterfall. Once you're across, it's time to tango with Hiyoihoi—Tokotoko who flings Ganchans at you. If you're not Super Mario, you've got virtually no chance of getting past the monster. Though there's a Ledge above Hiyoihoi, you can hitch a ride on Ganchan after Ganchan, edging closer each time, and then leap up. (Fortunately, if you die here, you go back to where the power-up was located!) The way to get through is to leap the boulders and shoot the albino with ten Super Balls. If you're Super Mario *and* desperate, you can waste your power-up by taking a hit from a boulder as you literally run through Hiyoihoi,

4/1: Bop the three ?'s for Coins, then go left and go down the Pipe, skewing right as you do so, or you'll miss the Coin Ledge. If you stay above ground, there are Coins in the first three ?'s and a power-up in the Block on the left of the next row. The second inverted Pipe contains a Pakkun Flower nipping down at you; the upward-opening Pipe after it also contains a Pakkun. If you don't have Super Balls, move past the first when it withdraws, wait until the second Pakkun goes down, and move on. (There's nothing in the Blocks overhead here.) You'll find Coins in the next two Blocks, but a Pionpi comes hopping at you from the right. These beings can only be stunned for five seconds by leaping on them; shooting them with two Super Balls is the one way to make sure they stay dead. If you're unarmed, stun the little fellow and move on,

hurrying past the Pakkun Flower to the next t
?'s, which also contain Coins. Keep in mind th
the Pionpi will follow you until you board the E
vators.

Leap off the second Elevator onto the two
Blocks, going down and clearing the Coins fro
them between shots from the Cannon on the rig
Get onto the Cannon, hopping onto the row of
and clearing the Coins from them when the Pioi
is headed left. When you leap the Ledge, you'll
greeted by another Pionpi and a bomb-toting Turt
get the latter before the former arrives. The thi
Blocks immediately overhead contain nothing, I
the sole ? on top has multiple Coins. Don't leap t
Pit immediately: wait for a second Pionpi to arri
Wait until he's gone to the left, then proceed. W
did you wait? Because the next Ledge is a duplica
of this one, except that there are *two* Nokobons
deal with. If the Pionpi hadn't come over, he wou
have been waiting for you there! The Blocks ab
you contain nothing; the single ? on top has j
one Coin. Wait and, again, let a Pionpi come ov
from beyond the Pit to the right, so that you oi
have to deal with one Pionpi when you get ther

Cross the Pit to the Pipes: the third and fou
contain Pakkuns, and there's a Cannon in the fif
Worse, the Pionpi will cross the Pit and come af
you. So, hop the Pipes as soon as the Pakkuns
down, get on top of the Cannon, and jump to
last Pipe in that row—it's the tallest one; the Gi
won't hit you up there. Across the Pit there's a P
kun Flower in the second Pipe and a Pionpi just

the right of it. Hop onto the Pipe when the Pakkun goes down, kill or stun the Pionpi, scroll him off the screen by hopping onto the first Pipe—he won't return—then double back and clear the Coins from the three ?'s overhead. Hop on the Pakkun Pipe when the Flower goes down, get on the last Pipe, and leap onto the Elevator. The first Elevator moves diagonally to the upper left, the next to the upper right. They're a piece of cake. You'll come to five Pipes in a row: one opening up, two opening down, another up, and the last armed with a Cannon. The first four all contain Pakkuns, so proceed using the stop-and-go technique—making sure that after the third Pipe, you hit the last Block on the overhead Ledge: there are multiple Coins—then jump onto the Cannon Pipe when the weapon is down.

There's a Pakkun in the next downward-opening Pipe; hurry past it when it withdraws and wait. A Chibibo will come by, and you'll want to get rid of it before continuing—taking care that you don't jump up into a Gira from the Cannon. Once the mushroom top is slain, do stop-and-go past the Pakkuns in the Pipe; when you come to an overhead Ledge of breakable Blocks, hit the last Block for a power-up. Once again, stop-and-go past the Pakkun Pipes, the first and fourth of which open up, the middle two opening downward. The last Block on the Ledge overhead contains multiple Coins. (Just watch out for the falling Block, like those you dealt with in 1/3.) When you've cleared the next two Elevators, you'll have to cross a series of breakable Blocks *fast* and then avoid the Cannon in the sec-

ond Pipe and the Pionpi beyond. Land on the Ca
non, bop the little man, and continue right, leapi
the next Pionpi and defeating the two Chibibo
(There's a power-up in the lone Block overhea
wait on the Chibibos if you need Super Balls, g
them, then blast the little critters.) Leap onto t
Elevator on the other side and jump onto the Ledg
you'll fine a power-up in the Block above. A thi
Elevator will take you to a Ledge; jump from it
the Ledge on the right, then up to the left, to t
L-shaped Coin repository above. Be careful, thoug
when you return to the Ledge on the right af
reaping the riches: to the right are *three* Canno
firing at you from three different heights! It'll
necessary to jump from the top of one Cannon
the next, taking care not to step on the Chibi
marching sentrylike after the second Cannon.
ter you clear the last Cannon, three Pionpis w
charge at once on the other side; shoot or bop '
fast. There's a Coin in the ? atop the row of th
Blocks, and three more Cannon after that, firing
different heights as before. The only difference
that there's no Chibibo here; deal with them as
fore. You'll see the Elevator to the right; before y
jump onto it, note where the Cannon are firin
they'll have changed direction because you'
passed them. Plan your move accordingly, goi
from the Elevator to the collapsible Blocks and i
the room at the top of the Tower.

4/2: Begin by leaping the Ledges over the wat
there's no danger until you reach the two ?'s ov

head. There's a Chibibo on the Ledge beneath them. Poise yourself on the right edge of the Ledge above the Chibibo and shoot it or drop onto it. Scurry to the right before it explodes, then go back to the ?'s and collect the Coins. Repeat this procedure at the next Chibibo . . . though you'll also have to keep an eye on the Pompon Flower below. It isn't difficult to avoid . . . as long as you don't rush ahead. Wait until the Flower is on the far *left*, then do as before, with one exception. After you bop the Chibibo, *rush* to the right and hop onto the row of ?'s. The reason? A Cannon is firing from the right, and will nail you if you dally. After the Gira has passed and the Chibibo has exploded, hit the ?'s for power-ups. Leap up to the Ledge on the right and drop down on the top of the Cannon. There's a Chibibo to the right, but that doesn't matter: you're going to go down the Cannon Pipe, and the Turtle will be gone when you emerge.

It's vital that you have Super Ball power in the Pipe, since there are 200 Coins in here and *no* Blocks. You can clear out half of them without Super Balls—some by from the ground, others by leaping off the top of the exit Pipe—but the weapon is a *big* help. When you reach the Dragon, hop onto the Ledge level with it, to the left, and jump up. This will cause the monster to fire its flame up, leaving the way clear for you to leap to the right and bop it on the head. After the Dragon, bust the Wall with the Chibibo behind it and collect the goodies up there—all Coins, save for a power-up, second Block from the left. If you aren't Super, you

must stay below, and you'll find Pakkun Flowers
all the down-facing Pipes. Go through them usi
stop-and-go, but scroll the screen *slowly*: when y
reach the Wall on the right, you're going to hop
to the left to get some of the goodies on top. Wh
you go back to the Wall, be ready to leap down fa
a Cannon to the right is firing at you.

You'll travel through an identical set of Pip
with Pakkun Flowers—plus the Cannon that w
firing at you—after which you'll reach another
ries of Ledges: there's a Chibibo on the Ledge
the upper right, and a Pompon Flower below
Leap onto the bottom-center Ledge when you c
leap over the Pompon (this is not difficult) and
the power-up from the left Block above you. Th
it's time for some fun with a new menace: t
Sparks. These are little fireballs that orbit Bloc
in a counterclockwise direction. (In general: for t
Sparks on the ground, it's safe to stand directly
either side of the central Block, or on top of it. T
Spark won't touch you here, and you'll definit
want these havens as you edge your way throug
Hop over the first Spark, then watch out at the s
ond one, located above: there's a Pakkun Flower
the Pipe below it. Wait until the Flower is do
and the Spark is moving away, then leap the P
and hug the right side until you can move past
third Spark. A Chibibo is waiting beyond this o
kill it, then approach the fourth Spark, which a
has a Chibibo patrolling under it. Wait until
Turtle has moved to the right before going after
kill it, then return to the ? that was the hub of

fourth Spark. (The Spark will be gone, having been scrolled off the screen to the left.) Bop the ? and get a Star, which should last you through the next Dragon.

After you get the Star, you'll cross a pair of horizontally-shifting Elevators, after which there's another power-up in the ?, which is the hub of the first Spark on this side. There's a second Spark, and another set of horizontally-shifting Elevators; watch when you jump off the second Elevator or you'll hit your head on the overhead Block and fall in the water. Wait until the Elevator is *all the way* to the right before getting off. Also beware the Chibibo waiting for you on the other side. There's an Invisible Block with a Coin directly above the Pipe to the right of the lower Elevator. When you reach the Dragon, deal with it as you did the previous one. You'll pass two more Sparks. Kill the Chibibo on the Ledge above, get down when it explodes— and also to avoid the Spark—continue past the second Spark, and you'll face a third Dragon. After defeating it, run across the widely spaced Blocks using the B button technique, making sure you stop after the last Block so you don't run into the Pakkun Flower in the downward-facing Pipe. When you reach the end of the platform, get to the *very edge* and jump up and slightly to the right when the vertically-moving Elevator is down. If you're not on the edge, you won't be able to get on the lift. Upon getting off at the top, you'll notice there's a breakable Block in the Bridge. Step on it and fall with it, skewing Mario to the right as you do so. If you

don't shift him to the side, he won't land on soli
ground and will perish. If you need more time t
study your surroundings as you fall, simply hop up
even though the Block is dropping, it's still soli
Climb to the top of the Tower.

4/3: This level's a lot like 2/3 in terms of strategy
like that round, this one scrolls, inexorably, an
you're borne along with the wind. The only differ
ence is that you should play in the middle as soo
as the Rocketons start appearing: they not only fir
forward, but also backward. You'll want to giv
yourself some extra maneuvering room to avoi
their missiles—which, alas, are immune to you
own blasts and also survive the scrolling-off or de
struction of the ship.

Very few of the Blocks contain useful object
There are power-ups in the first and fifth Block
overhead, and a Star two Blocks later, overhea
Indeed, it's a good idea to play this round entirel
in the upper half until you reach the maze: there
virtually nothing of use below. It's easy enough
shoot at the Blocks on top, since you'll be firing i
that direction to kill enemies anyway! When yo
first enter the maze, hang to the left until you clea
out the four foes that attack. They can go throug
Walls—you can't, of course—so beware! Enemi
will only appear in the first few corridors of th
maze. After they stop attacking, you'll enter a ma
sive Coin room. When you've cleaned it out—yo
have to do this by touching them: your bullets won
garner them here—drop to the bottom, shoot th

lower right-hand Wall, and continue. Your course after shattering the Wall will be right, up, right, down, right, up, right, down, and finally, right. What's important here is that you stay to the right, and go up and down vertical corridors as quickly as possible: the screen will scroll you left faster than you think! Fortunately, there are no enemies in here to distract you. When you exit, you'll have to face three Sparks: one alone, at first—simply stay on the bottom to avoid it—then two, one atop the other. You can pass the second two, as well, by staying on the bottom. However, when you roll into their domain, you'll want to go up: there's a two-Block wall on top, and the upper Block contains a power-up. You'll definitely want that so you can take a hit and not perish in the climactic two showdowns. Get the Coins above you to the right, then watch out for the enemies lurking in the two downward-opening Pipes: a pair of massive mailed Fists. *Don't* delay going through them: if the screen scrolls too far, you'll be *forced* to the right, and not necessarily at the best time. Head forward the instant the Fists go back in the very first time.

Once you've passed these, you'll shoot through a Wall and face the evil Blokinton, boss of this level. As soon as you've gone through the Wall, stay in the upper half of the room, firing ahead; you'll get in a few licks before the cloudlike creature attacks you. You must hit the Cloud twenty times to destroy it; the task is complicated by the vehicles that constantly emerge from the Cloud in pairs. Blast these, and stay directly in front of the puffy thug—

that is, to the left—whenever you can. Go to th
right of Blokinton, and above or below it, only whe
it heads left; if you don't, it'll pin you to the le
Wall and kill you. Then, as soon as the Cloud shif
back to the right, get on the left side of it again an
continue firing. When Blokinton is history, go t
the lower right corner, open fire, and get set to ba
tle Tatanga himself. The villain is nestled insic
the "war robot" Pagosu, which rises from the flo
and launches projectiles that divide, each piece a
celerating and fanning out at you. Though thes
can be felled by a single shot, they keep you fror
hitting your main target. Stay in the upper left co
ner of the screen, moving up and down only slight
to avoid the projectiles while you get in your sho
at the big boss. It'll take at least two dozen dire
hits on Pagosu's cannons to disable the ship ar
release Tatanga's captive, Daisy. (And, of cours
bring on the credits scroll! Speaking of which—co
grats to programmers M. Yamaoto and T. Harad
and director S. Okada, for an absolutely terri
game.)

After you win, press Start and the game will b
gin again . . . though not exactly as you remer
bered it! Though all the goodies are in the san
place as before, your foes have multiplied rath
significantly. For example, you'll find a Fly at th
first 1-Up in 1/1, and a Gao—yes, a Gao!—perch
atop the first multiple Coin Block. Bunbuns atta
right away in 1/2, there are more falling Bloc
than before in 1/3 . . . and wherever there was or
Gao in that level the first time around, there a

now two. A pair of Tamao work with Dragonza-masu at the conclusion of 2/3—though that won't affect your strategy at all—while you'll be greeted by a Cannon in the first Pipe of 3/1 ... and so on. Fortunately, you get "continues" if you lose at any level the second time around. (The continue mode actually begins in the closing levels of the first game. For instance, if you make it to Blokinton's chamber and lose your last Mario, you'll start level 4/3 again with three continues.)

When you become super proficient at *Super Mario Land*, you'll even be able to execute level select. All you have to do is make your way through the game *twice*. (Are there batteries that last that long?) After you do so, a prompt will ask you to select the round and realm you wish to visit. Make your choice with the control pad.

If you're having trouble with the game, you can earn as many lives as you wish ... assuming you have time and patience. In level 1/1, after you collect the first Star, continue to where the three rows of Blocks give you eight Coins. When you've collected these, leap off the cliff to the right, losing a Mario. When you return, you'll be right underneath the Block where you got the Star. Repeat this process as often as you like! The Heart will keep replacing the life you lost, while those Coins keep on accumulating, giving you extra Marios. (Just don't take a power-up: Super Mario, sans Super Balls, can't get the Coins nestled in those narrow corridors of the Wall at the end of the level.)

Finally, do the following at the end of world 1/1:

if you get into the top of the Tower, hold down the
A button while the time-remaining is being added
to your score. *Keep* the button pressed as you ship
into the bonus stage. You'll be rewarded with three
extra Marios almost every time.

SUPER MARIO BROS.

jective:

   Forget Disneyland: the happiest place in the universe is the Mushroom Kingdom, a land ruled by the benevolent Mushroom King and Princess Toadstool, his delightful daughter (despite her name). Unfortunately, the serenity of the Mushroom Kingdom is shattered by the arrival of King Bowser and his army of evil Turtles known as Koopa Troopas and Koopa Paratroopas. The ensuing war is won by Bowser, who uses magic to transform the conquered Mushroom People into Blocks and Plants. Worse, he imprisons Princess Toadstool—the only one with the power to liberate the tyrant's unwilling subjects. But all is not lost! With your help, bold Mario will attempt to reach the castle in whose dungeon Princess Toadstool is incarcerated, and free her. (If a friend is playing with you, Mario's brother Luigi will join him on his quest.) The journey will take

you through eight different worlds comprised of fo[
levels each.

Gameplay:

Some of the vilest life forms in the universe mal[
up Bowser's army, and there are three ways Mar[
can beat them: he can jump and land on top of the[
bop them by hitting up under Blocks on whi[
they're standing; or blast them with firebal[
(When you jump on a Koopa, its Shell can becom[
a weapon; if you leap on it again, the Shell w[
zoom along the ground in the opposite directio[
cutting down enemies like they were bowling pi[
Just make sure you don't get in the way if the Sh[
ricochets, or you'll die!) As Mario makes his w[
through the kingdom, he obtains various power-[
items that either materialize in the air or must [
uncovered by shattering Blocks. The Power Boost[
Mushroom transforms Mario into Super Mar[
while the Starman makes Mario or Super Mar[
invincible for just about a half minute. Fire Flo[
ers, which only Super Mario can obtain (Mario ca[
jump high enough to get them), give him fireb[
power. All power-ups move to the right when th[
arrive or are uncovered, though they change dir[
tion upon bumping into something. Blocks come [
four different varieties: Breakable Blocks, U[
breakable Blocks, ? Blocks, and Invisible Blocks[

Mario also obtains Coins as he plays. These p[
vide him with additional lives when he's collect[
enough. Some Blocks contain one Coin, others t[

Coins; these will be noted below in *Strategies*. Beware of Blocks, however, when you're about to do battle: if there's a Block overhead when you try to jump on a foe, you won't have enough room to clear your adversary. As a result, it'll run into you—in which case, kiss one Mario good-bye.

If Mario dies, you don't lose the Coins or points you've amassed. Where your next Mario begins depends upon where the previous one perished. Any enemies you've killed will return exactly as before—but the good news is you can re-collect Coins from Blocks. An important note: when Mario stands on a Block or Ledge, it isn't necessary for both feet to be on solid ground. Indeed, to bop up under certain Blocks, it's often necessary to situate Mario on the surface below so that one foot is standing on air!

In addition to running and leaping, Mario has the ability to crouch and squeeze through narrow passageways, which is accomplished by running (with the B button) and, when you reach the tight corridor, by pressing the controller down.

nts:

The prices on enemies' heads range from 100 to 1000 points. Some characters are worth more points depending upon how they're slain. Buzzy Beetle goes from 100 to 200 points if dispatched by an invincible Mario; a 100-point Koopa Troopa doubles in value when fireballed or hit by invincible Mario; a Koopa Paratroopa is worth 400 points instead of

100 points if you jump on them—which is only fa
it's tougher to get on top of the fly-guys. Ditto t
Lakitu, whose point value increases from 200 to 4
if you pounce on them. Points are also awarded si
ply for busting Blocks in Walls or ceilings, and 1
collecting Coins and power-ups. Even if you ha
that particular power, go for the item: you'll st
get points for it.

Other ways of earning extra points from destr
ing enemies are: killing two foes at once (that
with one jump); hopping from one right onto a
other (each successive leap doubles the score :
your previous victim); using a Koopa Shell to
down foes (see *Gameplay*, above); and stomping
foe, waiting, allowing it to revive, then rekilling
each new jump earning you increasingly high
points.

At the end of each level you get points for rea
ing the Flagpole, but you get far more points
when you leap, you grab the top.

A more daring way to earn bonus points is to
main on a Balance Elevator until the cable sna
and *then* leap off as the platform is falling. It ta
guts, but the 1000 points are worth the risk!

Speed matters in the game: points are also gi
for the number of seconds remaining on the tin
at the end of each world. The more time there
the more points you get.

ategies:

Before entering Pipes at any point in the game, consider where they're going to let you out. For example, take a look at the Blocks you'll miss out on if you enter the first Pipe in 1/1. Although you'll avoid danger, you'll also pass up a slew of important power-ups.

Here's a complete guide to each realm of every world.

1/1: From the beginning of this round to the *second* Pit, you'll face only Goombas. The first ? contains a Coin. There's a power-up and Coin in the next row, and a Coin in the ? above it. (Note: if you go for the power-up before you go for the Coin to its right, don't hit the Coin until the power-up has come down. Otherwise, by butting the Coin Block, you'll cause the power-up to roll to the left, right off the screen!) The first three Pipes can't be entered; the fourth contains Coins. However, if you enter it, you'll emerge just a few short hops from the end of the round, missing out on numerous goodies. It's recommended that you avoid the Pipe. Leaping over it, stand on the sixth Block from the left side of the Pit, jump up and you'll hit an Invisible Block which will give you a 1-Up. (If you decide to go down the Pipe, you can still get this 1-Up; just be careful not to scroll the Pipe off the left side of the screen.) Vault the Pit and get a power-up from the ? in the lower row of Blocks. The upper row consists of Unbreakable Blocks.

Jump the next Pit: in addition to Goombas, you'll

have to deal with Koopa Troopas here, so be pr
pared. Get a Coin from the ? on the top row, rig
the Block beneath it contains multiple Coins. T
rightmost Block of the next row contains a Sta
man. Four ?'s follow: the one on top is a power-u
and the bottom three are all Coins. The next tv
?'s you encounter (before the Staircase) are bo
Coins. Pass the second Staircase, then the thir
leap the Pit to the fourth, and cross over the Pip
(Note: this is the Pipe from which you'll exit if y
entered the other Pipe. While leaping on t
Goomba here, don't forget to get the Coin from t
? in the row overhead.)

1/2: You'll enter a Pipe to begin. Until you pa
the first row of eight Walls, you'll only have to d
with Goombas. (A cinch; in fact, you can mash t
first two with one jump!) The row of ?'s imme
ately overhead contain, from the left, a power-
and then all Coins. When you reach the Block af
the sixth Wall, you'll want to get the multiple Co
from within. However, before you do so, get on t
of the Wall and jump down, flattening the Goom
beneath the Block (at this angle, your fireballs w
be ineffective). After the last Wall, there'll
Goombas and Troopas underfoot. When you rea
the overhead Wall, jump up and break the Bloc
on the left side so you can collect the Coins ov
head. But don't leave until you've also hopped
and down under the Wall on the right side: the l
Block on the top has a Starman inside!

Facing Goombas and Troopas, you'll reach a a

ries of blue Walls. Get the Coins ahead. If you prefer to travel along the ceiling, free from danger, you
can do the following: as soon as you reach these
Walls, stand under the right side of the leftmost
Wall and break the three Blocks overhead. Hop onto
the Ledge to the right, jump up and bop the two
Blocks of the Wall overhead, leap left onto the remaining part of the first Wall you pounded, jump
up and shatter the Block overhead, in the ceiling,
and jump through the opening. You won't reap the
Coins below, but you'll get a breather. The ceiling
route will let you off at the first Elevator, discussed
below. If you remained on the ground: when you
come to the next Coin—a single Coin sitting on a
Ledge—get it and also break the Block beside it to
get a power-up. The Wall to the right of this has
multiple Coins in the bottom right Block. Get onto
the Ledge by the Pit and jump onto the Coin Ledge.
At the right side, stand on the last Block and leap
straight up: a 1-Up will sprout. As soon as it does,
break the Block beside the Mushroom, let it drop,
then grab it. Below, you'll be battling only Goombas until after you pass the Elevator—which will
be in a few moments. Enter the first Pipe and collect the Coins; make sure you also bop the Block
two Blocks in from the exit Pipe: there are multiple
Coins here. You'll exit not far from where you entered, and will have missed nothing ... except a
few Goombas!

Leap the two Pits, battle the Goombas, and wait
when you reach the Staircase: let the Goombas descend and crunch them before climbing. Cross us-

ing the Elevator, then position yourself under th
right side of the overhead Ledge: the last Block co
tains a power-up. Board the second Elevator, h
off onto the upper Ledge—actually, take a migh
leap right off the screen!—and walk along the r
to the Warp Zone. (If you missed the upper Ledg
jump to the left, back onto an Elevator, and t
again. The only time this *won't* work is if you lea
too far right when you got off the Elevator, in whi
case it will have scrolled off the screen.) The Wa
Zone consists of three Pipes which, from the le
will warp you to four, three, and two, respective
If you want to fight your way through the game, g
off the elevator and enter the Pipe. When y
emerge, you'll be at the end of 1/2.

1/3: Leap the two Pits to the Mushroom, getting t
Coins on top. (Note: the Troopa on top won't co
down, so you can deal with it when you ascen
When you leap to the next Mushroom, the Goomb
will come after you, so bop them as you go. Wh
you reach the high Mushroom overlooking t
floating Coins, get the Coins as you leap to the n
Mushroom, board the Elevator, hop onto the hi
Mushroom with the Coins, then drop down and
the ? for a power-up. Hop to the next Mushroo
and then prepare to do battle with the Paratroop
These airborne Turtles can rise *and* fall, so leap
top of them *quickly* to destroy them as you hop fr
Mushroom to Mushroom. There are Coins above t
two horizontally-shifting Elevators, which you c
nab as you slide by. Go from the narrow Plateau

the larger one, watching out for both Troopas and Paratroopas there and on the next Mushroom (the one covered with floating Coins). Two more Mushrooms and a single horizontally-shifting Elevator complete the level.

1/4: This is the level where you first meet the rotating Fire Bars. These little delights spin in different directions, and will sizzle you with their touch. You encounter one of these within moments after beginning the round. It moves in a counterclockwise direction, and you should jump over it when it's between the ten and nine on the clock. Leap it, then hit the ? for a power-up, vault to the right to catch the booster if you're Mario, or get on top of the Block to get it if you're Super Mario. The next three Fire Bars come one after the other, all moving in the same direction as the last one. Scoot under the first when it passes the three position, stop and wait for the second to do so, then wait for the third. You can actually take all three at once, if you time it right. Be careful, though: after the third is another Fire Bar moving in a *clockwise* direction. If that fourth one isn't in a favorable position, don't pass through the third until it is. Two more Fire Bars await side by side, the first moving counterclockwise, the second clockwise. Ideally, you should wait until the first is upright and the second pointed straight down; you can jump over the first and run under the second.

You'll be facing the boss of the level shortly, but the monster's presence will already be felt due to

its flaming breath. Make your way forward wi
care. When you come to a drop in the floor, st
down: there are a half-dozen Invisible Blocks, ea
of which contains a Coin. Jump when you've walk
a few steps, then get on top and take a power
one-foot-off-the-Block leap to the right to reach t
next (hopping fireballs as you do). Go down, take
few steps, jump up, uncover the low Block, get
it, and repeat. Do this for the next Blocks as we
After getting the six Coins, shoot Bowser with fi
balls. If you don't have any, you can wait until
shifts positions and leap over him or rush und
him. In either case, you must get to the Axe on t
other side. Use it to cut down the Bridge, and th
demon is history. If you're Super Mario, you c
also run *through* the fiend. It'll cost you your Sup
status, but during the few seconds it takes for y
to change from Super Mario to Mario, at lea
you're invincible and will be able to get the A
(Note: this Bowser, like the ones you'll be fighti
at the end of each level, isn't really the mas
Bowser, but an imposter—a Goomba, to be preci
You can only reveal the phony's true identity
killing it with a fireball. For the record, the succ
sive false Bowsers are a Troopa, Buzzy, Spiny, La
itu, Blooper, and the Hammer Brothers. The l
Bowser you face is the genuine article!)

2/1: Until the Staircase, you'll only face Goomb
Passing under the row of unmarked Blocks ov
head, break the one in the middle: it contains
power-up. There are Troopas after the Staircase, b

you'll want to stay in their lair just a bit because of the row of Blocks overhead. Jump to get a Coin from the Invisible Block to the left of the row. Leap *onto* that Block and jump up to reveal another Invisible Block: this one will give you a 1-Up. Nothing much lies ahead—except Goombas and Troopas—until you pass the next Pipe. The ten ?'s overhead contain Coins, save for the Block on the lower left, which will give you a power-up. Continue until you reach a single Block, then get on top of it, stand with one foot over the right edge, and leap up to the right, under the leftmost Block, butting it to reveal a Starman. Invincible, proceed over the Pipe to the two rows of ?'s, all of which contain Coins. Now, instead of leaving the ?'s, remain on top and position yourself at the right edge of the row on the left. Jump up against the Blocks overhead and you'll cause a Beanstalk to sprout. Climb it for the Sky Bonus, which consists of rows of floating Coins that you can only reach by hopping on a Cloud Elevator. It moves horizontally along the length of the Coins, allowing you to hop and grab them as it moves to the right. If you happen to fall off, you'll miss a few Coins—but you can salvage the trip by running to the right, ahead of the Elevator, and jumping back on. When you're finished here, just fall off and you'll land near the end of the realm.

If you stayed on the ground, there's danger . . . but riches as well. After leaping the Pit and landing on a Goomba Ledge, hop into the Pipe and collect the Coins therein. When you emerge, climb to

the top of the second Pipe you encounter: the left
most Block contains a power-up. After the nex
Pipe, you'll encounter Troopas and, on the othe
side of the Pit, Paratroopas. Upon jumping the nex
Pit and hopping off the wall, you'll battle Paratro
pas *and* Goombas; the Ledge overhead (not th
Block to the left of it—which, not so incidentall
contains multiple Coins) is the one on which you
land if you took the Sky Bonus route. The ? to th
right has a Coin, the Block to the upper right of
contains a power-up. The latter one's really toug
to get if you're Super Mario: you're just too big
fit easily. The best way to bump the Block is
start running while you're under the row of Block
where you alighted after your sky journey. Jun
onto the ? without breaking your stride, then jun
again and hit the Block. Your timing must be pr
cise, or you won't pull it off. There are Troopas
the other side of the Pipe, and they'll make it toug
to get to the Springboard. However, that litt
trampoline isn't the only way to get to the top
the Wall on the right. Leap onto the row of Bloc
overhead, then hop up and uncover an Invisib
Block with a Coin. Get on top of that and you'll
able to vault the Wall. You've made it to the e
of 2/1.

2/2: This is an underwater world, complete wi
Coral to snag you, Whirlpools to drag you dow
and new live foes. Your fireballs work just fine her
though, and that's good: they're the only thing th
will stop your first foes, the Bloopers. Even bett

the Bloopers don't go all the way down to the sea bottom, which means that Mario is completely safe strolling along down there, and Super Mario only needs to duck to avoid them. Nothing much happens apart from run-ins with Coral and Bloopers until you reach the first Pit. There are Coins floating above, and a Whirlpool below; to cross, hold down the A button—using Turbo, if you have the NES Advantage—and pump the button like mad! After swimming through the break in the Wall on the other side of the Whirlpool, you'll be attacked by both Bloopers and Cheep-Cheeps; the latter, like their comrades, must be fireballed to be stopped. When you reach the next Pit, watch out for the Whirlpool and also for the Blocks overhead: if you bang into these, you may get bounced down into the suction. After this Pit, you have only Cheep-Cheeps to worry about through the end of the level. You'll encounter a third Pit moments after the second; it's more challenging than the two that came before, because of the lips that partly cover both sides. If you go down to get the Coins, the exit is much narrower, requiring great navigational skills! There's nothing to obtain, and just the Cheep-Cheeps to avoid, between this point and the Exit Pipe.

2/3: A new form of Cheep-Cheep welcomes you to this Bridge level: the Flying Cheep-Cheep. While fireballs are, again, the best weapons to use against these creatures, they can also be stomped if you're agile enough to get on top of them! You'll find nothing but floating Coins and the Flying Cheep-Cheeps

as you cross the first five Bridges. The sixth Bridge
offers a power-up inside the ?, after which there
naught but Coins and the airborne fish for the re
of your journey here. Watch out for the sho
Bridges at the end: it's easy for a novice to ove
shoot these and plunge into the void below.

2/4: The living fireballs, Podoboos, make their d
but on this level. Fortunately, you don't have
decide whether to duck the goons or fight: they'
indestructible, so your only option is to hop the
when they appear, do your business in that are
and get out as soon as possible! They begin appea
ing as soon as you leap onto the first Ledge y
encounter. While avoiding the Podoboos, jump
the Ledge on the upper right, go to the right si
of that Ledge and hit the ? overhead for a powe
up. Jump from this Ledge to the next one on t
right, and prepare to pick your way past the Fi
Bars. These are rotating in a counterclockwise (
rection, so leap the first one when it's pointing
the imaginary nine o'clock, wait for the next (ove
head) to hit three, cross the third and fourth on
at nine, then wait until the fifth one (overhead)
a three. There are Elevators beyond this one, t
first set heading up, the second traveling down .
and a Fire Arm waiting for you on the other si
(bottom). Time your jumps so that you get off t
last Elevator when the Fire Arm is at the ten p
sition. Also, before you jump on the first Elevat
make sure you're standing exactly at the edge
the right side of the platform—the one with the fif

Fire Arm overhead. If you're too far to the left, you'll hit your head on the Fire Arm Block when you make your jump and plummet into the Elevator shaft.

As soon as you've gotten off the Elevators and cleared the last Fire Arm, the fake Bowser's fire will start rolling in your direction. Avoid it while you collect the floating Coins up ahead, crouching to get your Super Mario under the Block so he can claim the Coins on the bottom. This time, if you don't have Fireballs, Koopa's going to give you a little more trouble than before: there's a Ledge in front of him, which means you have to exercise more caution when leaping the fiend. Again, do this when he moves, get the Axe, and chop down the Bridge.

3/1: The two Paratroopas who attack at the very beginning are easy enough to slay. Do so, then get a Coin, Coin, and power-up, respectively, from the three ?'s overhead. The second Pipe you encounter leads to a a Coin room—obviously, don't jump on top of the Pipe until the Piranha Flower goes down. Inside, you must do the following in this order: stand under the overhead Wall on the left, jump up, and shatter the two lowest Blocks of the Wall. Hop up to the single Block on the right and nab the Coin there; you can probably grab the Coin to the right as well. If you didn't, go down and break the Block it's sitting on, then hop back onto the Block where you got the first Coin. Jump up and shatter the two Blocks directly over you. Take a powerful diagonal leap to the upper right, and break the Block for power-up. Clear out the remainder of the Coins working the right side of the room any way you wish.

When you emerge from the Pipe, you'll cross Bridge where you'll be greeted by a trio of Goom bas. Blast or stop them, then go to the right side the Bridge: if you're Super Mario—and only some times if you're Mario—jump up and uncover an Invisible Block with a 1-Up inside. Be quick about getting it, though, since it rolls to the right in hurry. Jump the Pit, stand on the bottom step, an hop up against the Ledge overhead: the leftmos Block will give you a Starman. Rush through th Goombas and Troopas, leap the Pipe, and do battl with the Hammer Brothers. You'll be able to blas the first one easily enough, but the second Hamme tossing Turtle will hop to the upper levels of th two Ledges ahead. Either bop him off—tough, give the continual rain of Hammers—or hang to the lef wait until he comes back down, and fireball him Get the Coin and power-up from the left and righ ?'s in the upper row.

Now, go back down to the ground, run hard, an jump up to the lower Ledge of the two Ledges ahea avoiding the Springboard. The trampoline will ge you to the upper Ledge, but that isn't what yo want. Sandwiched between the two Ledges, jum up under the Block on the right and you'll cause Beanstalk to grow. Climb it to the Sky Bonus an reap the Coins as you did before. If you can't mar age to get up there, use the Springboard to get t

the top Ledge, hop right to the Staircase, dispatch
the Goombas, and climb. When you leap from the
Staircase to the other side of the Pit, you'll have to
fight Troopas, Paratroopas, and Goombas. Between
bouts, get a pair of Coins from the two ?'s in the
Ledges on the left, a Coin from the upper Ledge on
the right, and a power-up from the lower Ledge
on the right. The Ledge you come to is the one on
which you'll land when you drop from the Sky Bonus. The second Block from the left on this Ledge
contains multiple Coins. Leap the Wall, jump over
the Pit, climb the Stairs—you'll be fighting Troopas
here—and you've made it.

3/2: The enemy population is heavy here, with
Troopas and Goombas both; it's advisable to kick
the Shells of dead Troopas to make headway. You
won't encounter any Blocks for a while; the first
appears after the floating Coins, and it contains a
power-up. Afterward, there are plenty more Troopas
and Goombas to occupy you. When you reach the
low Walls with a pair of Blocks floating between
them, up above, leap from the left Wall to the top
Block, get the Starman in there, then go for the
multiple Coins in the lower Block. If you try to do
it the other way around, Troopas will feast on your
bones!

After you jump the Pit beyond the right Wall,
you'll find no rewards: just Troopas, Paratroopas,
and Goombas. Deal with them as you did at the
beginning of the round. Leap the next Pit and carefully jump the Wall; if you jump too high, the Block

on top will knock you into the Pit to the right. (Th
Block, by the way, is empty.) Troopas only will do
your steps until you reach the floating Coins, afte
which they'll be joined by Goombas. Climb th
Staircase, jump down, and you're ready for—

3/3: Leap onto the first Mushroom and wait ther
until the Goombas drop from the second Mushroon
jump up and crush them. There are tw
horizontally-shifting Elevators: ride the first to th
second, and jump either to the Coins floating abov
the Mushroom, or to the Mushroom to the right
it, and just hop down. Jump to the Mushroom o
the right, get the floating Coins, then obtain
power-up from the ? on top of the next Mushroom
watching out that the many Troopas here don't na
you. Get the Coins on the lower right, then jum
up to the ? again and leap to the high Mushroo
on the right. Get the Coins there, then board th
Elevator to the right . . . keeping in mind that a
soon as Mario steps on it, the lift will fall like
wingless Paratroopa! Leave it quickly—taking ca
to land on the high, thin Mushroom to the right.
you land on the ground, you're sunk: there's no wa
off.

After collecting the Coins on top of each Musl
room, jump onto the highest one and go from ther
to the Balance Elevator. Like the scales of justic
these tip one way when Mario is on them. Get o
the left side, hop onto the Mushroom between th
Elevators, then jump to the one on the right. Lea
this one as it falls, jumping onto one of the tw

Elevators shifting horizontally to the right—one of these two is high, the other low; get on whichever is nearest. Hop to the thin Mushroom to the right, get onto the horizontally-shifting Elevator beside it, and collect the floating Coins from the three closely-set Mushrooms. Watch out for Paratroopas, which arrive as you prepare to hop the Pit to the next Mushroom; fireball them before you jump, or else bop them with extreme caution. Go from the thin Mushroom to the wide one, which is covered with Troopas; get onto the horizontally-shifting Elevator to the right; cross another Balance Elevator, and you've won the level.

3/4: This one's a toughie. Not only are there Fire Bars spinning counterclockwise over the Pits you have to jump, but those same Pits are disgorging Podoboos. There are four Pits to clear, guarded by three Fire Bars; leap each bar sometime after it's passed the ten position *and* when there are no Podoboos gushing out. (At least there are no walking, leaping, or flying monsters here!) You'll come to a Ledge of ?'s: from the left, you'll find a Coin, power-up, and Coin in them. To the right, you'll find something a whole lot more unpleasant: three pairs of Fire Bars. The first two on top are moving counterclockwise, the bottom two clockwise. The last set is going clockwise on top, counterclockwise on the bottom. The only way to make it through is to watch the movements of each pair of arms, leap between them when there's room, stop, and examine the next set before proceeding. The key is to keep your

eye on the top Fire Bar: if you jump high enough
you can leap the bottom one when it's at most any
position. Just make sure you've got the room on top
before you do so—that is, be certain the Fire Bar
up there is out of the way. Another quartet of Pits
lies ahead: no Fire Bars this time, only a steady
stream of Podoboos as well as the fire from the mock
Bowser at the end of the level. All you can do is
jump with care and precision. When you face the
sham Bowser, it's going to be tough getting over
him because of how *close* he is to the Wall that
blocks the Elevator. If you don't have fireballs
you'll need to be super skillful to avoid his blasts
get over him, and grab the Axe.

4/1: You're about to meet one of the game's most
taxing foes: a Lakitu, which slides back and forth
overhead, following you wherever you go and con
stantly dropping Spinys at you. When the Spinys
hit the ground, these horned Turtles shift back and
forth trying to kill you. To begin the round, hop the
Pipe to the right—when the Piranha Flower goes
down, that is—and you'll see two ?'s, one atop the
other. The Lakitu will appear as soon as you've
reached these. Get the lower one first: it's a power
up, and you may need it. Grab the Coin from the
on top, then *hurry* ahead, leaping the Pit and no
breaking stride as you jump to grab the floating
Coins above. The Lakitu will be ahead of you; while
running, fireball any Spinys that get in your way—
you can't step on them, or you'll die. Upon reaching
the set of four ?'s in the sky, don't bop them . . . no

yet, anyway. Leap onto the lower left ? and position yourself on the right edge, with one foot off the Block, in midair. (Do this quickly: the Lakitu can drop Spinys right on the Blocks themselves!) Jump from there to the top right ? This will put you at the same height as the Lakitu. When it slides in your direction, hop up and bop it on the head to slay it. Take care not to miss, and especially not to fall off: there'll be so many Spinys around, it'll be tough not to land on one *or* get back onto the ? Block. Now you can clear out the ?'s at your leisure, all of them Coins.

After jumping the Pit, raid the Ledge of ?'s for Coins, then get on top of the Ledge, stand on the second ? from the right, jump up against the Invisible Block, and get yourself a 1-Up. Continue to the right, hopping onto the wall and leaping from it to get the floating Coins. Do the same thing when you reach the Pipe a short distance beyond it. No Lakitu will bother you during this stretch. Enter the next Pipe if you wish to avoid the monster's return; in addition to the Coins, there's a power-up in the Block atop the exit Pipe, though it's virtually impossible for Super Mario to fit under there. If you stayed aboveground, the Lakitu returns as soon as you jump over the treasure-chamber access Pipe. Run and grab the floating Coins, get on top of the two tiers of ?'s, and again crown the Lakitu when it floats by. All of the ?'s contain Coins, save for the third Block from the left on the bottom row, which has a power-up. The Blocks directly over the Pit contain nothing.

Leap the next Pipe—this is where you would'v
emerged if you'd entered the Coin room—blastin
any Spinys in your way as you leap the two Pit
and hop onto the Wall ahead. There, you can tr
and battle the Lakitu as before. This is also a goo
vantage point from which to launch fireballs at th
creature. Cross the Pit, climb the Staircase, an
jump down. The Block to the left of the Flagpol
contains multiple Coins, so go down and collec
them. When you're through, climb onto the Bloc
and jump back onto the top of the Staircase. Thi
will enable you to take a stab at reaching the to
of the Flagpole.

4/2: Don't breathe a sigh of joy because you've lef
the Lakitus behind. The Goombas will more tha
keep your hands full on this level, as will the Buzz
Beetles, which are impervious to fireballs. They ca
only be slain by getting squashed, hit by an Invin
cible Mario, or bopped off a Block by hitting it fror
below.

After entering the Pipe at the beginning of th
round, leap the three Pits, then hop to the top o
the Ledge in front of you. Slip down the vertica
passageway at the end, collect the Coins, and jum
up to break the Block on the far right of the li
overhead. You'll receive a power-up. Jump up int
the corridor on the right, but take care: Goomba
patrol here, and it's too narrow to do any seriou
bopping. Thus, as you proceed, smash the overhea
Blocks to give yourself room. (You'll also give you
self one thing more. No, not a headache: the fift

Block from the right contains multiple Coins!) When you emerge from the narrow passageway, you'll find three rows of ?'s: all contain Coins, except for the second ? from the right in the rightmost row, which will give you a power-up. Board the Elevator to the right and get off before it sinks. Stop where you are and pay attention: this is truly a magical area!

Position yourself under the right end of the Ledge and jump up. You'll reveal an Invisible Block and collect a Coin. Move slightly to the left and jump up again to uncover a second Invisible Block and a Coin. Go left again, jump up and bop a third Invisible Block and Coin, then repeat a fourth time. Return to the first Block you uncovered, jump on top, then climb onto the second and third Blocks. Hit the Block overhead to cause a Beanstalk to sprout, then use the last Block you exposed to get up to the vine. When you reach the Sky Bonus, clear away the Coins and climb the Staircase. On the other side is a Warp Zone, Pipes that you can use to fast-forward yourself to Worlds Six, Seven, or Eight.

If you're slightly demented (like us!) and want to struggle through the intervening worlds, forget about the Sky Bonus and continue through 4/2. You'll come to a series of Pipes. There's a Troopa after the first. Kill it, get on the Ledge, and jump just to the left of the second Pipe to obtain multiple Coins. A Buzzy follows the second Pipe. Slay it and leap up, just to the right of the second Pipe, to reveal a Starman. The third Pipe contains a Coin room, and the only reason not to enter is if you need

a power-up or want to Warp to World Five. If yo
do, stay on the surface. You'll battle a Buzzy afte
the third Pipe, and Troopas after the fourth. There'
a Wall, a Pipe, and another Wall, all of which mus
be hopped, after which you'll reach a downwar
moving Elevator. The power-up is located in th
middle Block of the second Ledge. Collect it, boar
the upward-moving Elevator, and get onto the cei
ing on the right. Follow it—endlessly, it will seem!-
leaping a second Elevator and ultimately reachin
the Warp Zone.

If you're still determined to stay on the groun
get off that upward-moving Elevator at the Pip
Ledge—this is also where the Coin room will let yo
out. Deal with the Troopas beyond, then hop th
next two Pipes and a Pit, climb the Staircase, lea
onto the downward-moving Elevator when it's
the top, then get off *at once* onto the Coin Ledge.
you fail at this and can't get up there, take som
consolation in the power-up you'll find in the lef
most Block of the Coin Ledge. Climb the Staircas
to the right: there's a Pipe to the right, and a Buzz
at its base. Edge to the right of the step and jum
with caution. When you land on the Pipe, don't tr
to get to the Exit Pipe with one jump: the chanc
are good you'll hit the ceiling and drop into the P
below. Instead, slide off the Pipe and land on i
right base, jump up to the Ledge on which the Ex
Pipe is sitting, and stroll in. Climb the Staircas
jump to the Flagpole, and gird yourself for a lev
that demands precision leaping! Take hear
though: you're halfway through the videogame!

4/3: The new twist here is that the Paratroopas fly up as well as down. At least they don't home in on you, making them easy enough to duck. Hop onto the first Mushroom, skip the super-high second Mushroom for the moment and go to the third—fireballing or stomping the Troopas there—*then* double back to the second. Go back to the third, get a running start, and take a mighty leap onto the fourth Mushroom—carefully avoiding those versatile Paratroopas here. Skip the short Mushroom below and go to the one beyond it, claiming the power-up from the ?. Then drop off to the left, to the lower Mushroom, get the floating Coins, and jump to the Mushroom to the right. To get the floating Coin beyond it, hop on the Balance Elevator and sweep it up when you sink. Don't try jumping for the Coin and returning to the Mushroom; you'll fall to your death.

Leap from the Elevator to the Mushroom and onto the other side of the Balance Elevator, grabbing the floating Coin while it sinks. Hop onto the vertically-moving Elevator beyond, and then, if possible, onto the one after that when it's ascending; that's the best way to get onto the floating Coins Mushroom on the right. (Besides, there are Troopas on the Mushroom below it, and you might not want to bother with them.) Hop to the Coin Mushroom to the right, fireball or stomp the Troopas on the Coinless Mushroom, then drop to it and destroy the Troopas on the Mushroom between them. Get the Coin, hop back up to the right, and

cross the series of three Balance Elevators. On
fairly obvious rule applies to all of the Elevator
don't try to go from the left to the right side whe
the latter is higher than the one you're on. Mor
over, if you miss this jump-off window, don't risk
super leap. There are Mushrooms in the center o
each set of Elevators; use these as stepping-stone
to the other side, if necessary. Upon clearing th
last one, you'll be on a Mushroom covered wit
floating Coins. No foes will bother you as you ho
across the remaining Mushrooms to the last El
vator. To reach the top of the Flagpole from th
vertically-shifting platform, wait until it reache
the top, press the B button for speed, and jump.

4/4: There are no live foes until the very end of th
section . . . but don't imagine that things are goir
to be easy here. (You *didn't* think that, did you
As you bound down the steps and hop the two Pit
you'll notice that there are two routes you can tak
upper and lower. Take the upper; the lower rou
is a dead-end from which there's no getting out. A
you set out across the top, you'll encounter six Pi
with incredibly narrow plateaus between ther
Press the B button and run over these; if you fa
you'll end up in the dead-end section below. Whe
you reach the large Pit at the end of this sectio
leap over and land on the bottom portion of the br
ken Wall ahead. Go from this to the floor ahea
then leap up the three successive Ledges to th
top. When you come to the first Pit, drop down, a
left, then drop down the Pit you'll find there. Hea

right on the bottom level. If you take any other route, you'll be dead-ended!

Travel along the bottom, watching out for the one Fire Arm turning clockwise as you go. At the end of this passageway, jump up onto the Wall, and duck into the Pit beyond to avoid the imposter Bowser's fire. See the Fire Arm right before the monster? It's turning clockwise. You're going to have to wait until the Fire Arm is between the three and eight positions, leap over the alien, and get the Axe. When you do, you'll have completed the fourth world.

5/1: A long, flat stretch full of Goombas and Troopas welcomes you to this new world; kick the Shells for extra points. Hop the first Pipe, the Pit Beyond, and the second Pipe, then cross the next plain, battling Goombas and Paratroopas. When you reach the Wall shaped like a lopsided L, hop on top and break the second Block of the Ledge above it. You'll get a much-needed Starman. While you're invincible, leap the Pit, trample the Goombas, and charge the Turtle Cannon, which is firing Bullet Bills. Since you're invincible, you can run right through 'em all! (In any case, if you step right up to a Turtle Cannon, it won't fire.) After clearing the Cannon, vault the Pit to the Wall on the other side. The field beyond is populated by Goombas and Troopas, after which there's a Wall with a Ledge to the right of it. If you've gotten to this point *without* being hit, you'll find a 1-Up on the right side of the Wall, below the level of the Ledge.

Leap the Pit, watching out for Paratroopas an
the Bullet Bills fired by a Turtle Cannon to th
right, then get on the Cannon and jump to the Pip
to the left. Enter the Coin room and clean it ou
thusly: get on the Block over the Exit Pipe, leap
the Ledge on the left, hop up to the top of the Coi
chamber, cross and jump onto the left Wall, an
drop from there, diagonally, into the Coin chambe
After collecting the wealth, get multiple Coins fro
the Block over the Exit Pipe—Super Mario will hav
a very tough time doing that. When you emerg
the Turtle Cannon will be to your rear and there'
be another to your right. Scroll the left Cannon o
the screen as quickly as possible, and get on top
the other Cannon to scope out the Paratroopa
here—then beat the wings off them as you hop
the nearby Staircase. Jump from the top step to th
nearby Wall to the Flagpole to end the round.

5/2: Things really start to heat up with this realm
which is easily the toughest one yet! Mount th
Staircase with caution: there's a Turtle Cannon o
top. Ascend between shots and get on top of th
Cannon to proceed. See if you can get the Floatin
Coins with a leap from the Cannon; if not, pick you
way through the Troopas on the ground and use th
Springboard up ahead—again, timing your sprin
to avoid the Bullet Bills. The Springboard will al
prove useful getting you to the Coin Ledge to th
right. In addition to the money, the rightmost Blo
of the top Ledge contains a power-up. Watching o
for Paratroopas, go to the Staircase to your imm

diate right. You'll have to deal with the Hammer
Brothers before you can ascend; this is tricky because they momentarily merge from time to time
at the top of the Staircase, making them invulner-
able. If you haven't got fireball power, you're going
to have to jump on them between axe throws. No
fun, that!

The pipe after the Staircase leads to an underwater world, which it's recommended that you
avoid. There are too many goodies on and over the
ground to obtain, especially in the Sky Bonus. If
you *do* submerge yourself, you'll face Bloopers for
most of your swim, and Cheep-Cheeps at the very
end. The twist down here is that there are Elevators over two of the Whirlpools; if you don't make
your crossing fast enough, the Elevators will push
you down. If you remained on the land—

There are Goombas between the Pipe and the
next Staircase, which is just a few hops away. Leap
from the top step to the Wall on the other side of
the Pit, then proceed slowly: the Hammer Brothers
stand guard at the bottom. After disposing of them,
collect Coins from each of the ?'s in the Ledge overhead. When you've done this, jump to the next
Ledge, collect the Coins, then drop off on the *left*
side. When you're on the ground, leap up next to
the right side of the Ledge to reveal an Invisible
Block with a Coin. Climb the Block, and jump up
against the left side of the Ledge overhead. This
will cause a Beanstalk to sprout. Climb it for a Sky
Bonus, and clear it out as you did the first one in
the game (2/1). When you're finished with this,

you'll land well ahead of many dangers! If you re
mained on the ground—

Leap the Pit to the right, aware that a Turtl
Cannon will be shooting at you from the other side
and that Paratroopas will be falling. After clearing
the Cannon, get on the Pipe—this is the Exit Pipe
from which you'll emerge if you took the under
water route. You'll have to fight both the Hammer
Brothers and Buzzy Beetles here, so watch out! The
best tack is to jump on the lower Ledge to the right
and butt the rightmost Block on top. Catch the
Starman as it emerges, taking care not to fall down
the Pit as you do so. Hop the Pit to the Wall, where
you'll be dealing with Bloopers and Cheep-Cheeps-
obviously, refugees from the underwater world! The
first Ledge you encounter has multiple Coins i
the Block on the left and a power-up in the one o
the right. (This is where you'll come down after
your foray into the Sky Bonus.) Get on top of the
Ledge and vault the Pit to the Ledge on the right
then take your pick: go up to the Ledge to battl
Troopas, or descend and fight Goombas and Par
troopas on the ground. In any case, head to the
Block before the next Pit and gather the power-up
Use that Block as a stepping-stone to the Coi
Ledge on the right, then look out before continuin
to the next plateau: Paratroopas await. Clear the
next two Pits and you're home-free!

5/3: This level introduces the new, lethall
improved Bullet Bills, which cover the *entire* gam
field! Be ready to get out of the way at a moment

notice. Hop to the first Mushroom and then to the second two-tiered Mushroom, stomping the Troopas into oblivion and gathering the Coins. There are Goombas on the next three Mushrooms, so be careful as you jump down to the skinny Mushroom on the right, then up to the next Mushroom and on to the one beyond that. Turn and jump left to get the Coins, landing on the Mushroom below. Go back to the high Mushroom and take a long jump down to the Mushroom to the right, catching the floating Coins as you do so. Use the vertically-moving Elevator to hop onto the Coin-laden top of the Mushroom, then *carefully* drop down to the ? at the left edge of the Mushroom below, get under it, and obtain the power-up. The next two Mushrooms are free of foes, but the third is protected by Goombas and Paratroopas. You have to build up a good head of steam on the first and second Mushrooms to leap the gaping Pit to the third; just make sure you don't hit any Paratroopas on the way over. If you want, try using the Turtles as mini-Ledges, actually bouncing off their Shells as you cross the chasm!

There are two horizontally-shifting Elevators to the right. When they pass under the floating Coins overhead, deftly leap up and grab them. Collect the Coins floating over the next Mushroom, then wait and have a look at what the Troopas are doing on the Mushroom to the right. Jump over there when you can and leap down to the following Mushroom, collecting the Coins and killing the Paratroopas that descend. The next two Mushrooms are devoid of enemies—except for the ever-present Bullet Bill—

and if you can leap onto the vertically-moving El
evator to the right, you can avoid the Troopas on
the ground. Hop from the Elevator to the Staircase
hurl yourself from the pinnacle, and get the Flag
pole!

5/4: Just what you needed: more Fire Arms! And t
start with, the first one you must face is nearly hal
as long as the standard Bowser-issue Fire Arm
Worse, the Pit beneath it contains Podoboos. So
leap onto the small Ledge to the left of the Fir
Arm when the clockwise-moving flames are at th
ten o'clock position and there are no fireballs spew
ing from below. Get onto the Fire Arm Ledge a
soon as it swings past one o'clock. Bop the ? over
head *fast* and collect the power-up. If you aren
quick enough and the Fire Arm is headed your way
you can leap onto the ? for sanctuary and take
short hop up when the flames come around. Ge
onto the Ledge to the right of the Fire Arm, an
hurry to the Wall just beyond it. There are an up
per and lower corridor ahead: both take you to th
same place, but there are fewer Fire Arms sweep
ing across the top corridor. Naturally, you're goin
to have to edge your way through the passageway
So you'll know, the first Fire Arm—which touche
only the bottom—moves clockwise, the second (both
moves counterclockwise, the third (bottom) rotate
clockwise, and the fourth (top), fifth (both), sixt
(bottom), and seventh (middle), all move counte
clockwise. Once you've gotten by these, there's on
more counterclockwise-moving Fire Arm to avoi

when you leap onto the Wall. Go past it when it's at the two o'clock position.

Two Elevators await, the one on the left moving up, the other going down. They're easy enough to cross, though you can't dilly-dally since you've got the Fire Arm behind you and another one—turning clockwise—on the wall ahead of you. When you jump to the Wall ahead, go to the right edge and wait: the Fire Arm behind you can't reach, and you'll want to have a look at the Pit beyond before continuing. There's a clockwise-moving Fire Arm in the center, with Coins above and below it. Wait until the Fire Arm is facing straight down, then jump across and grab the Coins on top. As the Fire Arm swings around, scoot to the left and collect the Coins on the bottom. Wait in the left-hand corner and, when the flames are once again pointing in the six o'clock position, hop over the Block in the center and jump onto the Wall on the right. Piece of cake. (Sure!) P.S.: while you're engaged in this undertaking, you have to watch out for Bowser's fire, which will begin coming at you the instant you get off the second Elevator. If you get sizzled by it, your derring-do will leave you looking like a derring-doughnut!

You're poised, now, on the Wall after clearing the Fire Arm. There are two Pits beyond, each with Podoboos. What's more, there are also Podoboos in the Pit beneath the pseudo-Bowser ahead. You're going to do a bit more stopping-and-going as you proceed, due to the little fire fellows; otherwise, it's business as usual to beat Bowser.

6/1: The super-pesky Lakitu returns this round
the only foe you'll have, beginning immediately a
ter you clear out the first two ?'s—a pair of Coins
and jump the Pit. Climb the Staircase quickly t
get high enough to stomp the critter ... going a
the way to the small Ledge at the top of the screen
if necessary. When the airborne pest is gone, g
under that upper Ledge and hit the Block on th
left for a power-up. Descend to the Ledge on th
right and bump up under the Block on the right f
multiple Coins. Drop to the ground and race ahea
leaping the Pit, grabbing the floating Coins, an
hurrying up the Staircase—again, to stay on top
your foe. Jump over the Pit, again scooping up th
floating Coins as you go. Hop onto the inverte
L-shaped Ledge, and vault from there to the ta
Staircase beside it. Use this vantage point to de
with yet more of the dogged Spiny-spawning foe
then drop to the *lowest* of the two Ledges on th
right. Jump up: if you haven't been hit to th
point, you'll be rewarded with a 1-Up. If you ha
been hurt ... well, just try to be more careful ne
time!

Jump over the Pit and make your way onto th
nearby Pipe as quickly as possible; one guess wh
Lakitu attack! If you can't get the fiend from
here, leap to the right—grabbing the Coins as yo
go—and hurry to the Staircase. If you have tim
jump up just before you get on the Staircase, to u
cover an Invisible Block with a Coin. If you st
haven't slain the Lakitu, do so from the top of th
Staircase, then step onto the Ledge, jump to th

row of ?'s to the right, and drop to the Ledge below.
You'll get a power-up from the left ? and a Coin
from the one on the right. Leap the narrow Pit and
go up the Staircase, then down the three steplike
Ledges on the other side, using the top one as a
launch pad to stomp a Lakitu if necessary. Stop on
the bottom one and position yourself under the
rightmost Block of the middle Ledge. (If you're Super Mario, you'll have to press the controller down
to get the hero to squat, then inch him under.) Hit
up repeatedly for multiple Coins. When you're finished here, go right, jump the Pit, rush up the
Staircase, leap to the ultra-high Wall beyond, and
hurl yourself toward the top of the Flagpole.

6/2: There's nothing to find, and no one will attack
until after you pass the first Pipe. There's a Troopa
to the right: fireball or stomp it, then go down between the two Pipes and jump up. You'll reveal an
Invisible Block with a Coin. Get on top of that
Block, jump again, and you'll find a multiple Coin
Block. While you're doing all of this, be careful not
to scroll the left Pipe off the screen: once you've
collected these goodies, you're going back. Enter the
Pipe on the left and drop into a Coin room. Once
you've cleaned it out, exit; hop to the next Pipe,
battle the Paratroopas, go to the next Pipe, fight
the Buzzy beyond, and stand under the rightmost
Block of the Ledge overhead. Hit it for a power-up,
then jump onto the Ledge and up to the Pipe on the
right. You can go into the Pipe and visit an underwater world, or you can wait and access a Sky Bo-

nus; the latter is recommended. If you take th
seafaring route, you'll be fighting only Bloopers u
til after you've passed the two Elevator/Whirlpo
Pits and the two smaller Pits beyond. Then t
Cheep-Cheeps join the fray.

If you remained on the surface world, there a
Goombas on the other side of the Pipe, and abs
lutely *nothing* of value for a while. You'll pass u
der a Pipe built on a Ledge in the air, jump tw
small Pipes, leap a slightly larger one . . . and th
the good stuff starts. Stand between the Pipe y
just jumped and the one to your right, leap up, a
an Invisible Block will materialize with a Co
Climb onto the Block, and butt the rightmost Blo
of the Ledge overhead. A Beanstalk will appea
climb it and clean out the Coins in the Sky Bonw

You're a thrill-seeker and didn't go clou
hopping? Here's what you'll find on the groun
Jump from the Invisible Block onto the tall Pipe
the right, kill the Buzzy below, and pass over thr
Pipes until you reach the Pipe built on a Led
above you. Follow these directions carefully
you'll be Buzzy-breakfast, since there's an infes
tion of the creatures to the right of the next Pip
this, by the way, is the Pipe from which you
emerge if you took the underwater route. Jump on
that Pipe and leap up to the left, onto the right si
of the Ledge on which the "floating" Pipe is bui
Vault from there to the lone Block high overhe
then hop from there to the Ledge beside it. Fr
here, it's an easy drop to safe ground on the oth
side of Buzzyland.

There's zilch to be found in the next two Pipes, but you'll want to get on the second, jump to the Ledge on the right, and position Mario on the right side so that his foot is standing on air. Do a diagonal jump up against the left side of the Ledge overhead, and you'll get yourself a Starman. Jump to the Ledge on the right, drop down to the Staircase, and leap to the Pipe on the other side of the Pit. This Pipe leads to a Coin room, complete with a power-up Block over the Exit Pipe. When you leave, you'll be much farther along ... though we can't go there yet: if you took the Sky Bonus trail, it'll be letting you off right about here. Hence, beyond the Pipe is a Wall with Goombas on the ground to the right; the Ledges overhead are useless—except as platforms from which to attack Goombas. Once you polish off these creeps, you'll encounter a small Buzzy army under the Pipe built on a Ledge. That Pipe has nothing to offer, nor does the large one to the right. The next Pipe over is the one from which you'll emerge if you went into the Coin room. A trio of Pipes follows, after which Paratroopas guard the round's final Staircase. It's your call whether you want to zap them from the Pipe or the ground.

6/3: For the first half of your trek, you won't face a single living foe. But that doesn't mean you can take things easy—not by a long shot! After hopping across the first three Mushrooms, using the vertically-moving Elevator to collect Coins at the top of the screen—you'll have to hop up from the Elevator to snare 'em—and hopping onto the fourth

Mushroom, you'll need to make a *very* precise ju
from that Mushroom to a Springboard below t
horizontally-shifting Elevator above. Collect
Coins and hop to the next three Elevators, all m
ing horizontally ... but at different speeds, just
make your life miserable. If you have trouble g
ting from the first Elevator to the second, you c
drop to the Mushroom below, jump to the Mu
room on the right, and try to leap *left* onto the s
ond Elevator. Naturally, it's easier making
jump from Elevator one to Elevator two with
missing! The ? above the fourth Elevator conta
a power-up: time your bopping of the Block so t
you can catch the item as you leap from the fou
Elevator to the next lift, which moves vertical
You can rest for a moment on the Mushroom to
right of the vertical Elevator, then it's on to a
of Balancing Elevators. To get the floating Co
between the two platforms of the first Elevator,
at once to the right edge of the left platform a
hop to the right when the two sides are level,
lecting the money as you leap.

When you get off the second pair of Balanc
Elevators, try to do so when the right platform
high enough so you can get the floating Coins fr
the tall Mushroom. Leap to the Mushroom on
right, watching out for the debut of this level's B
let Bills. However, you can actually *use* the pro
tiles if you've got nerves of steel—or a brain of
clay. Hop two Mushrooms over and you'll see so
floating Coins. You *can* try going to the tall Mu
room two Mushrooms over and leaping to the

. . *or* you can wait until a Bill passes, leap up, and use it as a stepping-stone to fling yourself up at the Coins. It's a dangerous maneuver, but by now, hopefully, you'll have a few Marios to sacrifice in the name of adventure! Continuing from that tall Mushroom, there's a Springboard on the Mushroom below, to the right. Use it to get to the horizontally-moving Elevator above. (Don't jump from the Mushroom right to the Springboard: drop to the Mushroom on which the Springboard is resting and *then* hop on. You'll have much more control over how high and how far to the right you bounce. If you're smart, you'll go from that lift to the thin Mushroom below; if you're reckless, you'll try to jump right from the Elevator to the Balance Elevator beyond. Get the Coins between them as before, and try real hard to hop onto the tall Mushroom beyond. If you land on the small one, you're going to find it difficult getting to the Mushroom on the right. Once on that latter Mushroom, take a deep breath and hop quickly across the four Elevators to the right. These platforms don't move . . . until you step on them. (That Bowser's a real joker!) Then they plummet like a lead Mario. Obviously, you should try to sweep up the Coins by the second and fourth lifts . . . but not at the expense of a Mario! The fourth collapsing Elevator leads to a tall Mushroom from which the top of the Flagpole is easily accessible.

4: Aaargh! More Fire Arms await! You should be pretty good at slipping through these by now . . .

though leave it to Bowser to add a new twist to t
challenge! The Podoboos on this level come mo
frequently than before, while the ceiling in the F
Arm corridor is lower than you're used to! At lea
the flames on the bottom of the corridor all tu
the same way (counterclockwise). Only the eigh
and tenth of the eleven Fire Arms, situated in t
ceiling, move clockwise. Begin by leaping the fi
Pit and slipping past the Fire Arm when it hits t
three o'clock position. When the second Fire A
is at the nine o'clock position, jump the next Pi
Podoboos first appear here—bop the ? for a pow
up (getting on top of the Block if you need to esca
the return of the Fire Arm), then hop the next 1
doboo Pit. Just make certain that while you
watching the Fire Arm below, you don't accid-
tally leap into the Fire Arm turning on the oth
side of the third Pit. Use a stop-and-go technique
get through the corridor; as soon as you clear t
last Fire Arm, watch for the flaming breath of t
not-quite-Bowser. Duck into the Pit and unco
the six Invisible Blocks and Coins using the sa
pattern from the Pit in 1/4. Now all you have to
is beat Bowser to continue . . . a tougher task th
ever, since the shellhead is not only surrounded
Podoboos, but is tossing Hammers. (Just to give y
something *not* to look forward to, all the remain
Bowsers have that nasty habit!) You're going
have to do some fancy footwork not only to get
the Elevator above Bowser, but to *survive* up the
since the Hammers' arcs carry them to the lift.

rave and alert, get the Axe, and drop the annoying
creature into the Podoboo Pit!

/1: If you've had trouble with Bullet Bills before—
well, as Jolson once crooned, "You ain't heard
nothin' yet!" In fact, if you don't get along with
these creatures, you'd do well to go back to 4/2 and
warp ahead to World Eight! This realm's a nightmare! Not only are there ten—yes, *ten!*—Turtle
Cannons in this realm, but the second, fifth, and
enth are double-decker Turtle Cannons, firing two
parallel Bills at a time. The trick to surviving this
level is to get on top of one Cannon, jump over the
Bullet Bill coming from the next *or* leap down and
press down on the controller to duck, run toward
the next Cannon, get on top of it, etc. Oh—and while
you're busy doing all of this, you've also got to bop,
blast, or evade Paratroopas, which begin falling at
once.

The first part of the level—with the Bills and
Paratroopas—is pretty straightforward. Atop the
first double-decker Turtle Cannon is a Ledge, with
power-up inside the leftmost Block. You'll have
to be on top of the Cannon to get it. Following the
third Cannon you'll find four ?'s, all of them Coins;
the problem here is that the Paratroopas will corner you under the Ledge ... and, if you kill one
and toss its Shell, there's no room for you to jump
up when it comes ricocheting back. (Even if you do
jump, there are the Bills on *both* sides to worry
about.) Four Coins just doesn't seem worth the effort, but if you're determined to go for them, take

the two on the left and get out, cross over the Led
on top, then drop down and get the two on the rig
If you try to get all four in one trip, *somebod*
going to cream you! When you come to the Cann
located on an overhead Ledge, bop the Block to *
right of the central Block for multiple Coins
between Bills coming at you from the left and rig

Things get a *bit* less relentless after you leap *
Pit. The Hammer Brothers await on the other s
of the first Pipe. If you can't fireball them, you o
avoid them by *immediately* racing underne;
them, or you can wait until they come down fr
the Ledges and jump on to one to run past the
(There's nothing in the two Ledges overhead,
don't waste time looking!) Get onto the next Pi
leap up to uncover an Invisible Block with a 1-U
then drop to the right side of the Pipe to catch i
taking care not to scroll the Pipe off to the left,
get plugged by the Bills coming from the right. I
ter the Pipe and collect the Coins; when you e:
you'll have left the Cannon and some Troopas
hind. You're not quite home-free yet (you did
think you were, did you?): there's a Cannon to *
right. Actually, it's pretty easy to get on top of t
one and to leap, from there, to the Pipe beyo
Deal with the Hammer Brothers here as you
the ones before—again, there's nothing to get in
Ledges—hop on the Wall, go from there to the
of the Cannon, and jump onto the Ledge to
right.

There's a power-up in the single Block overhe
and a Springboard below to get to it. If you use

chances are good Bullet Bill will catch you in mid-leap. Instead, try standing on the right edge of the Ledge—one foot on thin air—and leaping up against the overhead Block after a Bill has come and gone. When you fall down after hitting the Block, skew Mario so that he comes down on the bottom of the Staircase to the right. Failing that, try to fall to the left of the Springboard; if you hit the Springboard itself, you may bounce right into an oncoming Bill! If you landed to the left of the trampoline, hop over it and the Pit to the Staircase. At the top of the Staircase, wait until the Buzzys on the next Staircase have gone to the ground, then leap across. Climb, hit the Flagpole, and move on!

7/2: Compared to the world you just left, this one is like a day at the beach ... literally. It's another underwater world, and there are no real surprises. The layout and menaces are the same as 2/2; if you got through that, you should have no trouble here.

7/3: The layout here is identical to 2/3, although there are more menaces. The Troopas first attack when you reach the second Bridge; you'll be beset by Cheep-Cheeps and Paratroopas on the third. It's recommended that you use the Troopa Shells to bash the foes up ahead. After the third Bridge and until you pass the Mushroom, you'll only have Troopas to deal with. The sixth Bridge has a ? above it, with a power-up inside. You won't be able to reach the Mushroom from here unless you go to the left a bit and take a running leap; make sure you get the floating Coins while you're in transit. After the first tiny Bridge, you'll face two Bridges guarded by Paratroopas. They don't go low enough to bother Mario, but Super Mario will have to kill them or do a lot of crouching to get by! Watch out for the underhanded, and underfoot, Cheep-Cheeps when you cross the three small Bridges near the end; they can butt you to your doom. Once you reach the downward-leading Staircase before the last pit, no other foes will attack.

7/4: This is a round of dead-ends, and if you make a wrong move—bye-bye Mario. But you *won't* make a wrong move if you follow these directions carefully. Do so, and the level will be a breeze. After walking down the Staircase, you'll come to two stationary Elevators which fall when you step on them. Obviously, get on and off fast, taking care to avoid the Podoboos spitting up from the Pit below. When you reach the Wall on the other side, go down and follow the corridor until you reach a thin Ledge overhead. Jump up onto it—*not* onto the one above—and, when you come to the end, hop up to the Wall ahead. Travel along it until it ends, then drop to the small Wall below. Hop up to the small Ledge on the right, timing your jump so that the Fire Arm doesn't charbroil you. Quickly leap to the Ledge above the Fire Arm—it can reach you here, so don't dawdle!—and then to the long Ledge beyond. Hop the Pit to the small Ledge on the right, go *down* to the Ledge below, go left, drop to the floor, and come right passing under the Ledge. Hop up to the *lower*

Ledge on the right. At the end of this Ledge, jump to the Ledge on the upper right, then drop to the Ledge below. Go left, drop off the side, come back under the Ledge, and leap up to the next Ledge on the right. Continue straight to the end of this long Ledge, then jump down. There's nowhere to get trapped now, so just move ahead, watching out for Bowser's fire. Again, Bowser's hurling Hammers now, so you'll have to deal with those . . . and, unfortunately, there's no Elevator to help you get past him. You're best bet is to run under him when he jumps, taking care not to get singed by the Podoboos below.

8/1: Here it is: the final world! The rules change here a bit. For one thing, if Mario dies, the next Mario isn't just set back a bit: he returns to the *start* of the region. Furthermore, you have much more territory to cross, but no more time in which to do it. In other words, you're going to have to hustle! And you're going to have to do it with far fewer power-ups available to you than ever before.

Goombas and Buzzys are the first to attack, and they do so immediately. After you pass the first Pipe, you'll have to deal with Troopas and cross five narrow Pits—hold down the B button to run over them without falling—with Goombas and Troopas waiting on the other side. Leap the tall Pipe and, if you haven't been hurt, jump up between the Pipes to get a 1-Up. Leap the Pipe to the right and the one beyond that, then drop down the next Pipe to enter a Coin room. Make sure you jump up one

Block left of the Exit Pipe to collect multiple Coins
When you leave—having avoided a herd of Goom
bas by going underground—you'll have to cross a
field of Troopas. Leap onto the next Pipe for a re
spite, battle the Goombas beyond, then hop onto
the Wall to the right. There's a long Ledge ahead
slip under it, dispatching the Paratroopas below
then leap up beneath the Ledge, below the second
Block from the right. You'll uncover an Invisibl
Block with a Coin. Jump on that and leap straigh
up again to collect multiple Coins.

Leave via the Wall on the right and cross the five
narrow Pits here, dueling Paratroopas as you go
When you reach the next Ledge, leap up to claim
the Starman in the third Block from the left. Rac
over the next three Pits, bash the Troopas beyond
and get atop the small Wall. Slip down to the othe
side and get a healthy running start so you can
clear the wide Pit ahead, grabbing the floating
Coins as you cross. Goombas await you on the othe
side, so start fireballing as you leap. Carefully ho
from Pipe to Pipe—there are three—then battle th
Goombas and Buzzys between the last Pipe and th
Staircase. It's a pretty long stretch, so be on you
toes! More Buzzys await on the other side of th
Staircase, along with two Pits: be alert when yo
jump the first, putting on the brakes—that is, press
ing left on the controller—lest you slide off the righ
side of the extremely narrow plateau between them

There are two Walls on the next plateau, wit
Troopas marching between them; they shouldn't b
much of a challenge. On the other hand, the super

narrow plateau between the next two Pits *does* post a problem. Run and leap hard *and* high so that you can use the controller to make minor course corrections as you descend. (If you can get the floating Coins over each Pit, great! But they certainly aren't worth risking Mario's life for.) Hopping from that narrow plateau isn't too difficult—certainly not as tough as it was getting *on* the plateau—and you'll make quick work of the Troopas on the other side. There are no foes after the first Pipe; when you pass the second, you've got some fancy jumping to do. There are four thin Walls, each higher than the last and with a bottomless Pit between them. There are no shortcuts: you need to do some Gold Medal-caliber jumping here, or you'll perish! When you reach the last Wall, take a long, hard jump and you'll hit the top of the Flagpole.

8/2: This level is the Pits . . . literally. And you also have Lakitus and other creatures to deal with, so gird yourself for a struggle! Paratroopas rain down from the word go and, when you leap the first narrow Pit, the first Lakitu shows its goggle-eyed kisser. Hence, get to the top of the Staircase as quickly as possible in order to crown the Lakitu and avoid the Paratroopas. But don't rest on your laurels: a Lakitu will dog you on the other side. Use the row of ?'s as a place to fight it, if need be. (There are Coins in all the ?'s; don't bother with them if you don't need them.) Cross the Pit and hit the Springboard so you can bash the Ledge overhead: the second Block from the left contains a 1-Up. As

you cross the next five Pits, there will be nothin
but those Pits and Paratroopas to bother you. Whe
you approach the sixth Pit—the one with the sma
Ledge overhead—a Turtle Cannon will loom to you
right. The best thing to do is get on that narro
Ledge and take a big leap to the top of the Canno
jumping any Bills that come from the next Canno
to the right—and also blasting the Paratroopas tha
will be falling. Get off the Cannon between Bill
run past the second Cannon, leap and hit the rigl
side of the next Ledge for a power-up, then get o
top of the third Cannon. Clear out the Buzzys ahea
for points, get on the Ledge to the right—jumpin
over incoming Bills from the right—and, in quic
succession, jump on top of the Cannon that is lo
to the ground, destroy the Buzzys ahead, stop a
long as you can under the Ledge with the Canno
on it, hopping up and down—the middle Block ha
multiple Coins—then take a big leap onto the Ca
non in front of you. Duck any Bills from behind a
you deep-six Paratroopas falling to the right, the
go over the Pipe that lies ahead. Hop the narro
Pit (easy!), get up on the Pipe, and—if this is yo
first time here—hit the Pause button and stuc
what lies ahead.

There are two narrow Pits and one vast one; cor
pose your spirit and wipe your palms before you t
to get across. When you begin your crossing, don
bother going to the first narrow plateau, but
right to the second; it's one less jump you'll have
take. After that, there's no way around it: you
need a hefty leap to get to the next landing. Fo

tunately, it doesn't have to be pretty or precise—just *long*. Once you're over, go into the first Pipe and collect the Coins in the treasure room. Use the same rather complicated pattern you used in 5/1, since this room is the same. Do so quickly, though: remember, time is short in the eighth world. Sadly, the Exit Pipe lets you out just a short hop from where you entered. Immediately ahead are Paratroopas and a Cannon; position yourself on the right edge of the Pipe, use the B button to accelerate, and take a huge leap at least onto the top of the Cannon—or, even better, over the Cannon and the Pit beyond it. The jump *can* be made. Just watch out for the Goombas—and the Bills coming from behind—when you land. Obviously, you should try to land *on* the Goombas rather than beside them. Climb the Staircase quickly—there's another Cannon ahead—and avoid the Buzzys below by jumping onto the top of the Cannon. Leap over the Paratroopas to the Staircase beyond, then carefully jump from the top step to the pair of Walls and the Flagpole.

8/3: We haven't talked much about the B (acceleration) button and using it in conjunction with the A (jumping) button to make truly miraculous leaps. But you'll need 'em both now more than ever before. With Paratroopas and Bullet Bills greeting you the instant you set foot in this realm, waste no time taking a Herculean jump to the towering Wall in front of you. Without slowing down, leap the Pit ahead—there's a Cannon in its depths—to the next

Wall. Stop at the right edge. There's a Pipe below
two Ledges to the right of it, and the ever-rotten
Hammer Brothers marching to and fro. Your goal
is the Staircase beyond—one whose *back* is facing
you (the stairs lead away from you, down to the
right). The fastest way to get to the Staircase is to
cross the top Ledge and drop down. If you travel
along the ground, you'll have to make an awkward
leap up and around the overhead Ledge on your
way to the top step. (You'll also be able to get a
power-up from the bottom Ledge, second Block from
the right ... but it's a death-defying route!) Wait
until the Hammers of the infamous duo aren't
reaching the top Ledge, or watch for a break in the
flurry—then B and A button your way to the Ledge
and rocket across to the Staircase.

Jump from the Staircase to the next fat Wall
ahead, and then to the two Walls beyond. Paratroopas will be falling all over the first two Walls,
but you should be able to handle them. When you
leap, try scudding across their backs to drop them.
Continue running till you reach the third Wall, after
which there's a thin, lower Wall beyond which are
two Ledges *and* the Hammer Brothers—virtually
the same setup you just suffered through. If you
want the power-up in the upper Ledge, get down
onto the lower Wall and hop to the top of the lower
Ledge when you can. The power-up is in the second
Block from the left. However, a wiser battle plan is
to take a power leap from the Wall you're on to the
upper Ledge and, from there, over the Pipe and two
Pits beyond to the next big Wall. When you alight

he welcoming committee will consist of Troopas ind Hammer Brothers. Keep the fireballs flying and ›e prepared to leap when necessary, and scoot ihead when you can. Cross the Pit to the next big Wall, where there are "only" Hammer Brothers to naul you. There's an Invisible Block a step in from .he right side; hit it for multiple Coins. The final Staircase is a pip: three floating Blocks and a small Ledge, with the Flagpole beyond. If you can build ip a good head of steam, leap right from the Wall o the top Ledge. Otherwise, you'll have to drop to .he ground and take the steps one at a time. Tricky ;oing, that!

8/4: This is it! The final level, the showdown with he real Bowser, and (fingers crossed!) the rescue of Princess Toadstool! In terms of layout, the level :ouldn't be simpler: just Pits and Pipes. But there ire no power-ups, and a slew of foes—but happily, 10t the Hammer Brothers—so put your senses on naximum alert as you proceed!

The first "delight" is a Pit spitting Podoboos. You :an't fail to notice it: the flames come up at you vhen you start down the first Staircase. A power ump from the top step to the other side of the Pit s recommended. Since time is short, leap the Pipe ind *run* here; there are no foes until after you ump the second Pipe. Blast or leap the Goombas here, then ride the horizontally-shifting Elevator across the Pit. Enter the next Pipe and you'll zoom ihead a considerable distance; when you emerge, get ›nto the next Pipe, kill the Buzzys to the right, leap

to the Pipe on the right, cut down the Paratroopas
you jump onto the Pipe beyond, then take a m
ment to assess the situation. You've got a Pit
your feet, Paratroopas beyond, and a mission to a
complish. See the floating Pipe ahead? When t
coast is clear, position yourself midway between t
Pit and the Pipe, jump up, and uncover an Invisil
Block. You'll get a Coin, but more important, you
be able to use that Block to get up to the Pipe. I
ing so, you'll cut a substantial distance from yo
journey *and* avoid a flurry of Paratroopas.

When you leave the Exit Pipe, step up onto t
Wall and watch out for the Cheep-Cheeps which l
gin attacking at the next Pipe to the right. As so
as you clear the next Pit, you'll find a Pipe th
leads to an underwater world. There is *no* bene
to going down here, other than to slay Bloopers
points. You won't find any power-ups, you don't
any mileage off your trek, and you'll have five na
Fire Arms to deal with—no Whirlpools, though.
in all, you'd be wiser to stay aboveground. If y
stayed out of the Pipe, you'll pass four more Pip
and then the Hammer Brothers will attack. If y
took a swim, they'll appear one Pipe after you ex
In either case, these Hammers are the elite gua
of King Bowser, who lurks not too far in the d
tance. There's no way around the Hammers exc
to go *through* them. If you lack fireball power, i
be awfully tough to stomp on them ... but yo
have no choice. Making the top of the Pipe yo
staging area is the best tack, since it enables y
to back off to the left if need be, to get additio

ieight when leaping the Hammers, and also to
iump on the Brothers' heads the *instant* they stop
hrowing their weapons. Finishing them off, you'll
iave to leap a Pit with Podoboos, after which it's
Bowser time! There's no new advice to offer regard-
ng the master monster; as in previous worlds,
you'll have to get under or over him—under is eas-
er—although his attack is somewhat more relent-
ess now. When you accomplish this, you'll be
rewarded with the real Princess Toadstool . . . and
he thanks of a grateful kingdom!

ting Notes:

n closing, here are some helpful hints and an in-
eresting sidebar.

Ever lose your last Mario and wish you could con-
inue in the same world? All you have to do is push
lown the A button and *hold* it down as you press
Start. This won't keep you in the same *realm* . . .
ust the same *world*. Still, it beats going back to
he beginning. However—

If you want to stay alive and thus avoid having
o continue, you can do so by having a slew of Ma-
ios in reserve. Back in 3/1 there's a Staircase with
Troopas at the very end of the realm. If you jump
into the *left* side of the last Turtle's Shell, that will
reeze it beneath you. Each time you leap up on the
pinned tortoise, you'll be rewarded with a 1-Up.
Just make sure you don't acquire more than 100
Marios in reserve, ever, or the computer will auto-

matically slaughter them *all*! (Must've been p
grammed by Bowser.)

Finally, you've noticed the fireworks that go
whenever you enter the castle at the end of ea
area? But did you know that the number
fireworks you get depends upon the last digit
your time remaining? If you end the round with
1, 3, or 6, that's how many bursts go off. Wha
more, you get 500 points for every blast! If you
any other number—sorry, no fireworks.

SUPER MARIO BROS. 2

ective:

Bowser may be gone, but the universe will never
ant for tyrants. This time the fiend is Wart, who's
ibjecting the world of Subcon to the monsters cre-
:ed by his Dream Machine. Heroic Mario and Luigi
olunteer to stop the wicked one, and this time
iey're not alone: they're joined by the brave Prin-
:ss Toadstool and Toad.

eplay:

s they venture through the seven worlds of Sub-
in—twenty levels in all—players can be any one of
ie four characters, which offer the following abil-
ies: Mario is an okay jumper who weakens slightly
hen he's carrying something; Luigi is a better
imper, but weakens more than Mario when he's
igging something; Toad is a so-so jumper, but
oesn't lose any of that ability when he's toting

something; and Princess Toadstool can levitate
nearly a second. The game is for one player or
although you can switch characters between lev•

There are many more weapons at your dispo
than there were in *Super Mario Bros.* The most
portant of these are:

• Mushroom Blocks: can be used to build St•
cases or to bop enemies.

• Mushrooms: power you up as in other Ma
games.

• Vegetables and Unripened Vegetables: use '
to bop your foes. Collect five vegetables and yo
earn a Stopwatch, which will briefly freeze your
versaries.

• Bombs: use them to blast creatures or Wa
but if you throw them too soon, they may not w•
the way you wanted, and if you hold them too l•
you may not work at all!

• POW: destroys all enemies around you.

• Rockets: ride them over your enemies.

• Turtle Shells: it isn't bowling for dollars,
bowling for survival as you find these under Gras
and use them to knock down beasties.

• Cherries: just hanging around in the air, th
can be plucked; get at least five of them, and yo
bring on—

• Starman: as in the previous game, he ma
you invincible.

• Potion: opens the door to Subspace, where
can reap all sorts of riches.

• 1-Ups.
• Coins.

One additional power that Mario has in this game
the ability to stomp most of his foes, then pick
em up and toss them at other creatures who want
trim his mustache. This power will be discussed
low, where appropriate.

s:

here are no points and no timer. (Phew! Who
eded the pressure?)

egies:

orld by world and level by level, like Henry V,
e go once more unto the breach! (Note: use Mario
r all of the worlds, except for the following: Luigi
r 2/1, 4/1, and 5/3, and Princess Toadstool for 3/1
d 4/2. To be candid, poor Toad isn't really a help
a any level . . . though you might want to give the
og a try whenever you know you've got to carry
tion a long distance, such as in 1/3.)

1: You're falling, but that's okay: there's a mul-
iered Hill below you. What's *not* so okay is that
ere are Shyguys on several levels. Fortunately,
eir population is pretty thin and you won't have
y trouble getting to the Vegetable growing on
e right side of the third plateau down. Finish up
ickly here and head to the door at the bottom

right of the screen. In the next room you'll f
these objects in the following order: a Vegeta
an Unripened Vegetable, and a Vegetable. The S
guys here are easily crunched. On the right sid
the big Hill, climb the Vine and claim the three
ripened Vegetables from the left, then pull the Pot
from the ground on the right. It will allow you
access Subspace, where, among the Coins, you'll a
get yourself a Mushroom. The thing about Poti
however, is that you should try and use it where
see the most Grasses; like Vegetables and other ite
Coins and Mushrooms are hidden beneath sprigs
Subspace. Since your time in this night-like dim
sion is limited, why use the Potion somewhere
and waste seconds racing to the Grasses?

Except for the hanging Cherries and an oc
sional Shyguy, there's nothing much happen
until you reach the next Hill. All of the Grass
here and on the Log Bridge beyond give forth
ripened Vegetables. After crossing the Log Brid
you'll come to a Waterfall with three Logs bobb
roughly side by side. Jump on these as you did
Elevators in the first Mario game. There are Un
ened Vegetables in the Grasses on the other sid
Bomb at the foot of the Hill, and a Turtle Shel
the ground to the right of it. After the next sn
Hill you'll find a Vegetable and then an Unripe
Vegetable. You'll find the same two items in
Hill just ahead . . . hardly worth the effort to
them. After crossing the next Log Bridge, yo
come to a door. Enter it. If you don't, you'll m
out on an exciting region—and a shortcut to a m

distant section of 1/1! When you enter the room via the bottom door, pull the two Vegetables from the ground, then continue *left*. Hop on the Wall and climb the Vine. You can also enter this room through the door on the second level of the Hill, to the right. There are no Grasses *inside*, but to the right of the room you'll find, from the left, Potion and two Vegetables. You'll have a Shyguy or two to battle up here, but the Potion will give you additional wealth—so it's your call. Whichever entrance you take, your next move will be to jump hard to the left to cross the Waterfall. Climb the Walls—disposing of the Shyguy there—and pull up either of the Grasses for a Bomb. Hurl it down the ladder, blowing up the Wall on the left. (Note: if you mess up during the procedure, leave the Hill chamber and reenter; everything will be as it was before you went in.) Go through the door in the chamber below and you'll be spirited to the end of the level. Just climb the *big* Wall to the left and you'll be ready for a showdown with the boss of this level, Birdo.

If you *didn't* enter the room in the Hill, you should still go to the upper level, pulling out the above-mentioned Grasses to the right of the door and continuing *right*. All the Grasses ahead of you are Unripened Vegetables, after which you'll come to a Vine. Climb it and get off on the Shyguy-infested, multitiered Hill. As you ascend, there are four Grasses to pluck here. From the bottom, they're an Unripened Vegetable, a Vegetable, and another two Unripened Vegetables. When you

reach the top of the Hill, hop up to reach the lowest
Vine, then climb, shifting to neighboring Vines
when Clouds get in the way. Keep an eye out for
the Vine-clinging creature, the Hoopster; it'll prevent your ascent if above you, but will help you up
if below you. Switch Vines in order to use the little
dream-thing to your advantage.

You'll know you've reached the top of the tallest
Vine: it stops, and there are Clouds to the left and
right. Go right, and you'll reach Birdo's Mountain.
Unlike the other route, which would have taken
you above and behind the boss, this one brings you
face to beaked face. The feathered fiend is going to
be tossing Eggs at you, but don't worry: leap up,
catch them by landing on them, and throw them
back. Three hits and the goose is cooked!

1/2: A new mode of transportation is introduced in
this level: Pidgit's Flying Carpet. As you begin the
round, it'll come bobbing along: jump on, and Pidgit
will vacate the premises. (Miss the Carpet, and you
won't be able to leave the starting gate!) The Carpet will be yours for ten seconds, during which time
you'll duck some Beezos (winged Shyguys) while
riding over a total of five Hills to the low plateau
beyond. When you get off, enter the left Jar for a
1-Up, then go to the left and pluck the Grass there.
It will give you Potion. (All the other Grasses on
this Ledge conceal Unripened Vegetables.) Throw
the Potion between the Jars and enter Subspace;
you'll get a Mushroom between the Jars. When you

exit the twilight realm, enter the Jar on the right and get the Key. Phanto will pursue you; get rid of the Jar denizen by putting down the Key for a moment, and the creature will go away. Head for the Hill to the right, watching out for Snifits, and use the Key to open the door.

Inside, the first five Grasses contain, from the left, a Bomb, two Vegetables, and two Bombs. More importantly, there are enough Cherries here to bring on a Starman ... assuming you grabbed at least two prior to this. Leap the two Pits, using your invincible body to plow through Snifits and Ninjis. Upon reaching the Ladder, climb, and *don't* pull the Grass to the right for Potion ... not yet. There are Bombs in the Grass to the left of the Ladder and to the right of the Potion Grass. Use these to blast the far right side of the Ledge, go back and get the Potion, and drop down. Use the Potion here for a trip to Subspace and the acquisition of a Mushroom. Exit the Hill chamber at the far right. Go *left* when you leave, pull out the one clump of Grass on the top of the Hill, and carry it to the *right*. Drop off the top of the Hill—still holding the Potion—to the lower Ledge, and use the Potion where you see all the Grasses. The Subspace will be *most* rewarding! Continue to the right, drop off the Hill, hop onto the big step you encounter, then enter the door. Birdo is on the other side, standing on a platform dead ahead. Well, not *quite* dead: you have to catch and toss back three Eggs. *Then* the wicked boss will be fricasseed.

1/3: If you have trouble leaping from one sma
Ledge to another, this level's going to be a nigh
mare for you! To begin, you're going to have to jum
three Pits between Hills. You'll want to stay on th
top levels to get the Cherries above each pea
though when you have to jump to the third Ledg
do so when the nasties on top are on the right. Gra
the Cherries, then quickly drop down to the lowe
Ledge to avoid them. You'll have to leap up fro
there to cross the next Pit, which brings you to th
Hill with the Log Bridge. The first Grass is an U
ripened Vegetable, but the next is Potion; use it o
the right side of the Bridge to get a Mushroom. Ho
to the next four, small Log Bridges and you'll reac
a Waterfall with three *very* narrow Logs bobbin
up and down. Cross them to the next Hill. (One sa
ing grace: if you fall from the Logs, there are na
row Hills below . . . last-ditch places to land *if* yo
can get to them.) There are Vegetables in th
Grasses atop the next Hill, but those aren't as in
portant as what lies beyond. Cross the two sma
Logs on the next Waterfall, and walk to the ne
Log Bridge. The first Grasses beneath it give yo
Potion—the second and third are Unripened Veg
tables; the Grasses on the Log are an Unripene
Vegetable and Vegetables. Take the Potion *back*
the Hill on the other side of the last Waterfall, an
use it on the top to obtain Coins *and* a Mushroo
Or—even better—you can carry the Potion to the J
ahead of you, to the right, and throw the vial ther
Subspace will open up; if you enter the Jar then, you'
warp ahead to the *fourth* world! If you don't—

Return to the Log Bridge where you obtained the latest Potion, hop the small Waterfall, and enter the door in the brick building ahead. You'll find yourself in the center of a long vertical chamber. Hop to the Ledge below you, to the right, go down to the right again, then ascend using the right side of the three successive overhead Ledges. Go left onto the Vine and climb, make your way to the next Vine (on the right), cross to the Vine on the left, go to the next two Ledges on the left, then go up to the Ledge on the right. Get the Key from the room at the top, then climb back down, past the point where you entered the chamber, to the door in the lower right. This will take you into a horizontal chamber populated by sundry enemies and, to start, Spikes right below the Ledge on which you're standing. You'll have no problem with these, assuming you can jump to the Ledge beyond! You'll hop across a total of five not terribly wide Ledges to three sets of Bridges, stacked vertically. You'll want to get on the middle group in order to get the POW just right of center. Six Ledges follow this section—though you can skip the sixth and drop down to the Ledge below it to avoid the Spark. (Just watch out for adversaries on the right!) Go right, through the long corridor, and you'll reach a Crystal Ball; get on top of it, and you'll find yourself in the antechamber of Mouser, the boss of this world. All the Grasses in this room are Bombs; not surprising, since you must blow up the Wall on the right to get to Mouser, and then use Bombs to destroy the fiend. Three Bombs will do the trick; you

can also catch the Bombs the giant rodent thro[w]
at you, and toss them back. The key is to try a[nd]
get behind the monster, where you'll be clo[se]
enough for the Bombs to do some damage witho[ut]
being endangered yourself.

2/1: You'll be slithered after by Cobrats during t[he]
desert portion of this level, so be prepared to kill [or]
jump them. Jumping is, in fact, something you'll [be]
doing a lot of here; the sand beneath you is qui[ck]
sand, and if you tarry too long at any spot, you['ll]
sink and die! Bypass the first Jar, which contai[ns]
nothing but a Snifit and Shells. (The latter are u[se]-
ful as weapons, of course, but you should *not* ne[ed]
them here!) When you reach the oddly-shaped W[all]
just after the second Jar, go up and get the Poti[on]
from the first clump of Grass—the others conta[in]
Unripened Vegetables. Use the Potion, but ta[ke]
care not to drop the Mushroom: it'll sink in t[he]
sands if you do! After the Wall, there's nothing b[ut]
Shyguys and desert until you come to the next Wa[ll]
which has a Panser shooting fireballs from the to[p]
(Suggestion: bop the Shyguy below and toss him [at]
the Panser.) Once you get by, cross more desert a[nd]
then a magnificent golden Pyramid will loom. Ent[er]

The Pyramid is filled with sand, and you mu[st]
dig down. Start on the right and, after a mome[nt]
you'll come to Cherries. Shift to the left and coll[ect]
more Cherries a little farther down. Burr[ow]
straight down from there for a third bunch of Ch[er]-
ries, then dig horizontally to the right for a four[th]
set. You *should* have enough, now, for a Starma[n]

which is good: Shyguys roam among the sands here, and invincibility will make your job a whole lot easier. Cut back to the left side and climb down the Ladder. Head to the door on the right, then exit the chamber and climb the Wall in the next room. Your old nemesis Birdo is waiting on the other side of the Pit: deal with the creature as before, but make sure, while you elude its Eggs, that you don't fall into one of the Pits.

2/2: You won't find anything new for a while after you pass through the door and begin the next leg of your journey: more sand, Shyguys, and Cobrats to start. Alas, the Jars hold nothing of particular importance . . . nothing *good* that is. Leap the first Jar you encounter and get on the plateau. The first clump of Grass will give you Potion—there are Vegetables in the others. Use it while you're on the plateau and collect the Coins and Mushrooms. At the end of the plateau hop from Jar to Jar, then hurry across the next plateau. As you cross this expanse, use the rib cage at the end as a Springboard if you need to keep yourself from sinking. When you reach the Rockpile, drop to the right and enter the door. You'll find yourself in a chamber with Grasses that give you a 1-Up (lower right), and Bombs (the Ledge to the left, above the 1-Up). Destroy the Wall, enter the room on the left, jump to the golden Wall, and get Potion from the Grasses second from the right on *top*. (The Grasses below, right and left, contain Vegetables; right of the Potion is a Vegetable, and left is a POW.)

When you leave the room, continue across t
sands with caution: in addition to the projecti
spitting Cobrats, you'll face Pokey, a troubleso
cactus. If you can't leap the green bein', grab
fallen foe—such as a Cobrat—and throw it at I
key's head. None of the Jars in this stretch of d
ert is any more rewarding than the ones befo
Your next challenge is a pair of Pansers sitting at
a golden Wall; either you can bring a bested enei
to throw, or you can race past them—your goal i
red Vine in the Wall beyond. Get on top of the sta
and climb *down*. It will drop you into a deep ve
cal chamber filled with sand, Cherries, and Sl
guys. Start digging toward the right side to get t
first Cherries, continue diagonally down to the rig
for the second batch, diagonally down to the left
the third, diagonally right for the fourth, and
agonally left for the last. Then go to the right si
and head straight down to reach the door. As y
make like a mole, remember: the Shyguys can or
move from side to side. The door opens into a cha
ber where you'll climb down a set of steps to t
right and—surprise!—you'll have to battle anotl
Birdo. Although you can still use Birdo's Eggs
clobber the villain, it's recommended that you p
up the Mushrooms on the bottom level, carry th
up the left to the Birdo platform above, and bo
bard the creature with those.

2/3: After climbing the Ladder back to the dese
head right and grab the first clump of Grass

Potion. Carry it to the left, past the Ladder, to the small Hill, and toss the vial there. Enter Subspace to obtain Coins and a Mushroom, then go right. The next Grasses you encounter will all be Vegetables. When you come to the Hills, you'll want to enter the door atop the first Hill on the left: there's a Subspace inside, with Coins and a 1-Up. In order to get up there, however, it'll be necessary to hop on the head of a Beezo and use him as a Springboard to reach the top. To get back down to the desert, hop to the Hills on the right—the Grasses there contain Vegetables. A *really* long expanse of desert stretches before you, and Beezo attacks occur with regularity. Your destination is another huge Pyramid; enter and you'll find yourself at the top of a loooong vertical chamber. Jump to the narrow Ledge on the *left* and fall, like Alice down the rabbit hole, to the sands way below. (If you go down the right, you'll face more enemies than on this route.) The instant you hit the sand, start digging. Again, you should burrow downward diagonally to reach the Cherries: first to the right, then left, then left again, then right, then down with a slight diagonal slant to the left. When you reach the last bunch of Cherries, cut to the left and you'll hit a door. Enter and get the Key, dealing with Phanto as you did previously.

Upon obtaining the Key, dig up to the top of the sands. To the right is a door; use the Key to get in. The new chamber is a pip. It's long, and the only power-ups are Cherries. When you reach the sand, dig down for the first Cherries, then dig straight ahead to the right for the next one back, diagonally down to the right for the third, and diagonally up to the right for the fourth. Leave the sand and, at the very end of this Pit, you'll find Cherries hanging overhead. This'll give you a Starman, enabling you to race past the Shyguys and Panser on the Hill ahead. There's nothing but more useless Jars, Cobrats, and other foes in the remainder of the chamber—nothing you haven't had to deal with before. However, when you reach the end and enter the next room, a new challenge awaits: the monstrous three-headed, fireball-spitting serpent Tryclyde. Actually, dealing with the monster is easier than it might seem. When you enter, you'll find six Mushroom Blocks stacked to the left of the two Ledges to the left of the creature. Form a barricade against the fireballs by stacking three Mushroom Blocks on the left side of the lower Ledge, and three on the right side of the upper Ledge. Then dismantle the lower wall you built, carrying each Mushroom Block to the top Ledge one at a time, jumping onto the wall you erected there, and throwing the Mushroom Blocks at Tryclyde. Hit the beast three times and it's a goner.

3/1: Enter the door and you'll find yourself on a Ledge halfway down the face of a raging Waterfall. Jump off the Ledge and literally drop to the bottom, where you'll find a door. Enter, and the room will offer two options, both involving Potion—tenth clump of Grass from the left; the others are all U ripened Vegetables. You can use it to collect Coins, or you can carry it to the far right side of the chamber and toss it at the Jar. Once you're in Subspace, you can enter the Jar and warp ahead to World Five. If you opt to stick around—leave the chamber by the door in the corner and you'll find yourself on the Waterfall on the side opposite the door in the Hill. Hop up and, when you reach the top of the cataract, get on Pidgit's Flying Carpet as you did before, in order to complete your ascent. Grab the Vine on top and climb to the Cloud Ledge where— if you're the Princess—you can float to the *left* to reach a secret doorway that will spirit you to the end of the level. If you're anyone else, get off the Vine on the left, have a look to the right to assess the situation—that is, where's the Shyguy?—then go right to the first Hill; your best bet for getting up there is to hop up onto the first Cloud to the right, jump up to the one on the left, move to the one on the upper right, then leap down to the Hill from there.

On the Hill are two clumps of Grass; the first contains Potion, the second an Unripened Vegetable. Use the Potion on the Hill, but be careful when getting the Mushroom: it, or you, may fall into the abyss beyond. After leaving Subspace, continue to the right, climbing the three Clouds and using the Mushroom Block on the third as a weapon, if need be. Drop onto the Hill and climb the next three Clouds. Leap ahead to the top of the two-tiered Wall—using the Unripened Vegetable on the lower tier (left) or beside the Ladder to deal with foes.

Climb down the Ladder, pull the Potion from the leftmost Grass—the others are all Unripened Vegetables—and use it here. The Mushroom will be outside the chamber; not only should you hurry to get it, you must take care: it, too, is on the edge of a cliff. When Subspace disappears, make your way to the door on the right. The Birdo you'll face here is a bit more versatile than the others: the Eggs don't move in predictable patterns, so you have to be on your toes to catch them. It's a good idea to get behind Birdo—go from the Wall to the upper Ledge and drop down on Birdo's Ledge—then bop the beast with the Mushroom Blocks you'll find there.

3/2: There's a world below your feet, but you can't get to it—not yet, anyway. Head right, picking your way through the swarms of Beezos; the only Grasses you'll find in this part of the world are two Unripened Vegetables on the far side of the first Hill. Some distance beyond that, you'll cross two POWs but *don't* use them: if you remove them and shoot to the level below, you'll miss out on the Subspace on the next (and last) Hill. Hop on top: from the left, the Grasses contain Potion, a Vegetable, and a Vegetable. Use the Potion, collect the Coins and Mushroom, and beware when you emerge from Subspace: a Snifit will be waiting to attack you. Drop off the Hill to the left and use the Grasses there—both Bombs—to blast away the Blocks in the ground to the right of them. Drop through the open ing, head left, and climb down the first Ladder you encounter.

Drop to the Ledge below you, hop up to the Ledge on the left, and pull the Grasses—all are Bombs—to destroy the Wall at the bottom of the Ladder. Destroy the next Wall to the left, then the two beyond that. If you need more Bombs, use the Grasses down here or climb the next Ladder to the left to the room above—a worthwhile trip, in any event: you also get a POW there. When you reach the left end of this section—you'll know you're there because you can't go any farther—jump to the Ledge on the upper right and climb the Ladder there. Go left, and descend the first and only Ladder you find. This will bring you to the other side of that Wall you'd run up against. Hop the three Pits to the left— watching out for a Shyguy attack—then climb the Ladder there. Cross the small chamber, climb down the next Ladder, and destroy the Block Wall to the left using the Bombs on the Ledge—there are three of them, and you'll probably need them all: the Wall is a sturdy one! Go through the next chamber and up the Ladder, but *don't* go all the way to the top. Just climb a few rungs, then go to the left. The Grasses, from the right, contain a pair of Vegetables, Potion, and Bomb. Use the Bomb, first, to blow up the Blocks in the floor on the right side, opening the chamber below; when you use the Potion to access Subspace, this is where the Mushroom will be. When you're finished here, climb the Ladder the rest of the way and enter the door in the middle of the room. Travel to the left for your next confron-

tation with the indomitable Birdo. This one's eas
to kill: just hop your foe, get to the Mushroo
Blocks on the left, and pelt the bird.

3/3: Upstairs you go, and through the door to
new adventure. The first Grasses you encounter
immediately after the POW—consist of Unripen
Vegetables followed by a Potion on the right. Wa
until you enter Subspace, get the Mushroom, ar
then get the POW: when you emerge from Su
space, you'll have *two* POWs! Except for the usu
flock of foes, not much happens until you reach t
door set in the side of the brick building. Enter ar
head left; from the right, the Grasses will give ye
a POW, a Shell, Potion, and another POW. Do
use the Potion here; carry it to the left. Sparks ar
Ninjis will attack you as you travel, but they ca
be stopped using the POWs. You'll pass below
door on a Ledge above—it's the first of three doo
on this level, and it leads to Room Three—then pa
beneath a second Ledge, and finally beneath a thi
Ledge. Walk past the next door and use the Potic
at the Ladder. You'll be able to get a Mushroo
from the Ledge above.

The second and third doors in this room lead
Rooms Two and One, respectively. (Got that? Do
One leads to Three, Two leads to Two, and Do
Three leads to Room One.) Entering Door One—t
door on the Ledge—you'll be in a tall, vertical roc
in which your goal is a doorway on the upper rig
Reach it by climbing staggered Ledges. The ea
going presents a whopper of a problem: the Jar

the fifth Ledge is producing Shyguys at an alarming
rate. Since you can't beat them all, you're advised
to avoid them: leap the little creeps, and shift to
the left or right to get out of their way. When you
reach the door, enter the small room and get the
Key ... taking care not to get creamed by the
Sparks or Phanto. When you're finished here, leave
the way you came and head to Room One—the door
on the left side of the chamber. Enter and ascend
this tall vertical chamber. Your chief foes in the
lower half of the room will be Sparks. Happily, you
won't have to deal with them for very long: slip
between them when you can, slowly but steadily
making your way up the "+"-shaped Ledges to the
silver Ledges to the door on the upper right. (On
the way up, after the + Ledges, there'll be a flat
silver Ledge, a rectangular one, then another flat
one, followed by the door.) Now ... if you avoid the
door and continue upward here, you will come to a
long Ladder. Unfortunately, when the Ladder ends,
there's no way to reach the Ladder on top of it—
unless you're the Princess and can float to it. So,
you have to leave the chamber via the door, enter
another chamber, and come back to this room
higher up, beyond the Ladders.

When you go through the door, you'll be in a new
room, a long vertical chamber; this is the room you
could have accessed by Door Two in the earlier
three-door room. You were directed to come *this* way
because it's the least dangerous route. Ascend using the silver Ledges—there will be five in all—then
head to the Chain on the left and climb. When you

reach the next silver Ledge, you'll notice a pair
Pansers to the right; they're bad news, becaus
you've got to cross the platform using the Chain
overhead . . . Chains sitting right in their crossfir
Just wait until there's a pause in their onslaugh
then make like Tarzan and rush from Chain 1
Chain as fast as possible. Climb to the top of th
last Chain, then cross to the left to the door. Pa
through it and you'll be back in the other roor
well above the Ladder section. Sparks await, but
do Cherries and Grass which contains a POW—th
latter is in the silver rectangle that will short
scroll into view in the upper left. Ascend using th
silver Ledges until you reach a Ladder just left
center. Climb it to the door on top, enter, and you'
be in a horizontal level.

The first and only Grass here contains a Shel
bring it to the level's only Ledge—which you mu
use to cross the chasm—and use it to bowl your e
emies over. When you reach the Crystal Ball at th
end, you'll enter the last room of this world: th
headquarters of boss Mouser and his guardia
Sparks. As before, catch the Bombs and lob a ha
dozen of them back at the big rat to destroy him.

4/1: Much to your chagrin, you'll find a new twi
here: ice! You'll be walking on it, so take care n
to slip. Playing Luigi, begin your trek and keep a
eye out for the Flurry or two you'll run into—c
rather, who will run into you. The first clump
Grass you'll encounter contains Potion: get it l
sliding under the Ledge above it, then hopping on

that Ledge after you have the Potion. Use the magic up there, but only when Flurry isn't nearby. Get the Mushroom, and continue to the right. The Grasses there all contain Vegetables, which will be extremely useful against the Flurries. After you go down the steps and jump onto the next platform to the right, you'll find Grasses on the right. (Note: the Ledge here is not slippery.) The clump on the bottom right contains a Vegetable; the two Grasses on top contain Potion (left) and a Vegetable. Use the Potion here and get the Mushroom from Subspace. When you emerge, go to the icy Ledge on the right and drop down. The clump of Grasses here will give you a Rocket. Take it: it's your only way out of this level.

The second stage gives you more icy Ledges to negotiate. In addition to Shyguy, you'll face its new conveyance, the Autobomb, which not only homes in on you, but spits flame. Your best bet is to kill Shyguy, then hop right on top of the Autobomb, letting it give you a piggyback ride. Do this again after the Wall: get on top of the Column, hop onto Shyguy, and ride the Autobomb. There are more Flurries, more Columns, and more ice ahead . . . but nothing that will cause you to lose any sleep. At the end you'll find a Crystal Ball but no boss; a charitable gesture from the otherwise merciless Wart!

4/2: Be the Princess this level: you'll save yourself a lot of pain. To get under way, climb the Vine and go right. The word "uneventful" accurately de-

scribes this part of your journey. Oh, there ar
Flurries and Beezos, and it's a good idea to get ri
of them the instant you encounter them: the Flu
ries will keep after you if you don't. But you shoul
be able to breeze through to the door at the en
When you get there, enter and you'll find yourse
in a considerably more difficult level. Drop off th
Cloud and go *left* to the Grasses, obtaining—fro
the right—two Vegetables and Potion. Now, if yo
enter Subspace from the back of the Whale, you'
find a Mushroom waiting for you. If not, you'll g
Coins. (Or, you can save your Potion and use
ahead, at the Jar. More on this in a moment.) F
ther way, head right when you're finished ther
making sure you get the Cherries hanging abov
the floating Ledges at the top of the screen. Th
next *two* sets of Grasses both consist entirely of U
ripened Vegetables, but the lone Grass on the to
of the next Wall will give you Potion. Again, ent
Subspace from a Whale if you want to get a Mus
room. Finishing up here, continue to the right.
you kept the Potion, continue carrying it until yo
reach the Jar. Use it here, enter the Jar, and you'
warp ahead to the Sixth World. If you don't do thi
go right to the Grasses, pull them out for a Rock
and ride to the next screen. There are Cherries b
hind the first Column, and the Grasses you'll e
counter will give you Potion. More important is th
corridor beyond them: it's lined with Spikes,
you'll have to board the Autobomb to get acros
Grab the Cherries as you go through and Starma
will appear, enabling you to walk right through th

Porcupo on the other side. The door at the end leads
to the Birdo chamber. Since the Ledge on which the
boss is standing is made of ice, you'd be wise to get
on the Ledge beneath and mount your attack from
there and from the low Walls on either side.

4/3: When you stroll through the door, there's a
Birdo to your right and Grasses on the roof immediately overhead and on the higher roof to the right.
The one on the left is Potion; Vegetables are in the
other two. When you obtain the Potion, go to the
Columns on the left: use the magic here and you'll
find a Mushroom on top of the centermost Column.
Return to the door, and instead of killing Birdo, get
on top of one of the Eggs and use it as a conveyance
to take you across the expanse of ocean to the right.
Otherwise, you won't get across: even the Princess
can't levitate *that* far! When you reach the Staircase Wall on the other side, all of the Grasses there
contain Unripened Vegetables. Leap over to the
thin Ledge on the right, then enter the door in the
Tower. (Note: even if you're the Princess, you won't
be able to vault to the next Ledge on the right.
You've no choice but to use the door.) Inside is a
vertical chamber; you must use the slippery Ledges
to ascend, leaping and bopping Flurries as you do.
Watch out for the Icicles (Spikes) on the Ledge halfway up; fortunately, they're the only ones you'll
encounter in this room. The exit is located in the
upper left. The door leads you to a Bridge between
the two Towers; you'll find Potion (left) and a Vegetable in the Grasses on the span. Take the Potion

to the *left*, climb the two Clouds to the top of th
Tower, go to the Tower on the right, and use th
magic there to obtain a Mushroom.

Upon entering the door on the other side o
the Bridge, you'll find yourself in a Tower similar t
the one you just left. Leave the Ledge on the lef
then stand at the edge of the Ledge you're on. Wai
until a Shyguy passes by, then jump on his head
it's the only way you'll get across the Icicles u
here. Drop down the Pit beneath the Icicles—nabbin
Cherries as you fall—and land on the Ledge i
front of the door right at the bottom of the Pit. In
side, you'll find the Key needed to open the door a
the bottom of the chamber. The Flurries in her
won't present much of a challenge. In fact, once yo
have the Key, you can use it as a weapon! Descen
along more icy Ledges to the door at the botton
just to the left of center, and use the Key to unloc
it. You'll find yourself in front of the second Tower
go right and enter the door in the third Towe
You're in a Crystal Ball room, but there's no boss—
not yet, anyway. Get rid of the two Flurries, go th
Mask door, enter, and you'll find a small room wit
the missing boss—the vile, fire-spitting Fryguy. T
combat him, use the Mushroom Blocks in th
room—preferably the ones on the floor. Grab on
and go to the left or right corner, heave it at Fr
guy, grab another and repeat. Three strikes an
he'll split into four mini-Fryguys; use the Mushroo
Blocks to hit and destroy these permanently—fro
the upper Ledges if you can, though the corners a
okay too.

5/1: The first level of this world starts out easy enough ... but then it really gets hairy! The first section offers nothing except foes—the most troublesome of which is the Panser shortly after the second Palm Tree. Getting past it between bursts, go to the end of the cliff, jump down, and hop the Pits to the *left* until you come to a door. Go in, and you'll find two Grasses right in front of you, and five clumps in the niche ahead to the right. The Grasses at your feet contain a Bomb (left) and Potion. Use the latter here for Coins. When you get to the top of the Wall, you'll notice that there's zilch ahead of you except for water and Logs. Guess how you're going to have to get across! After reaching the next Wall, you'll be faced with the most difficult challenge yet in the game: using the heads of your enemies, the Trouters, to hop across the Waterfall. You'll have to use a trio of Trouters to reach the next "oasis," another Wall. Use Logs to cross the next section of Waterfall, then Trouters, then stop when you get to the Wall with the Ledge above it. There are Grasses on that Ledge: a 1-Up on the left, Potion on the right. (Note: you'll have the easiest time getting up there if you're Luigi.) Enter Subspace and get the Mushroom from the Ledge below. Upon emerging from Subspace, continue across the Waterfall. The two-Log section at the end is the last you'll have to deal with—but make sure you deal with it *correctly*. There's a room ahead, but you don't want to go directly into it. When you're on the last Log, jump right and up: slide down the vertical passageway

in order to get the Mushroom Block stuck in the
center of it. You can't get this object from below.
Once you hit the ground, you'll find Grasses: Potion
is on the left, and the rest are Unripened Vegetables. Use the Potion here, get the Mushroom, and
head right. You're in Birdo land yet again. Since
the boss is now spitting fire, you have to be on your
toes—and on Birdo's case! Hop the creature, get the
Mushroom Block, and use it to bash the bird. You'll
have to hit Birdo three times with the same Block
in order to be victorious.

5/2: Travel to the right, climb the Ladder, and enter
a world of darkness! The first Hill has four Grasses
a Bomb (left) and three Unripened Vegetables
When you get to the Trees beyond, you'll notice
something unsettling: Hoopsters traveling up and
down the trunks. You can go under 'em when
they're up, or over 'em when they're down. (Over is
better: you can bop them!) Shortly after the first
group of Trees, you'll come to a lone clump of Grass
with a Vegetable, then a higher plateau with more
Trees. Beyond these Trees you'll find a Jar and
more Grasses. Surprisingly, there's no Potion in the
Grasses; from the left, there's just a Bomb, two Unripened Vegetables, and a Vegetable. Ah, but there
is the Jar! Enter with a Bomb, blow a hole in the
floor, and drop to a secret room below! There's a
clump of Grass and (voilà!) it's Potion. Take it, leave
the Jar, and use it when you're outside. At the end
of the plateau jump down to lower ground and continue right; there's nothing good here, so don't daw-

dle. Hop the small Pit to the next narrow little Hill, and use the Bomb from the Grass there to make the Tree enemy-free. Climb and jump to the next Hill, then be prepared to jump from one Tree to another—each of which has a Hoopster on it. It's best to make this double jump when the nearest Hoopster is high on the Tree and the second Hoopster is low: you have to go from the second Tree to the rather high Hill beyond, so you want to be able to climb if need be ... tough to do with the Hoopster coming *down* on you! There's a Pit and a *very* narrow Wall after the Hill, so jump to the latter with care. Get on the Tree beyond, and this time kill the Hoopster: you're going to need its carcass to bop the Panser on the next Hill. Get on the Panser-free Hill, jump onto the next Tree, and get to the Hill beyond. There's a small Hill rising from this larger one, and you'll find Grasses on it: two Vegetables with a Bomb sandwiched between them. All will come in handy here. After this nub of a Hill, you'll encounter two more Grasses: the one on the left has an Unripened Vegetable, and the one on the right a POW. After crossing the big Pit beyond, you'll come to a Vine. Start climbing, video-gamer!

As you ascend, a second Vine will appear to the left. Don't take it. Although a pair of Snifits and a Beezo will come at you, there's a Hoopster waiting on the left Vine: if you shift there, Hoopster will attack and you'll have nowhere to retreat. At least the Snifits (on the sides) and Beezo (comes from beneath you) can be dealt with rather easily. Get off

on the Cloud at the top of the Vine and go right
into the door. There's a Bridge whose center Block
is a POW: remove it and drop through. As you free
fall—quite a distance, so don't be alarmed—be prepared to shift left and right to avoid the Icicles that
poke up from cliffs along the way. When you finish
passing through the narrow neck of the canyon, begin shifting to the right. There's a Ledge with a
door; if you miss it, you stand a good chance of landing in the Trouter-filled waters and perishing. Going through the door, you'll find yourself in (ta-ta)
Birdo's presence. In addition to the typical Egg-
tossing contest, one really good tack to use here is
to stay to the left of the break in the Bridge, grab
Trouter when it appears, and toss *it* at Birdo.

5/3: As William Dozier used to say, "Another challenge for Luigi!" (Actually, he said it about the
Green Hornet ... but new times demand a new
hero!) You'll need Mario's brother's jumping skill
for this world. Go right to the Ladder, climb, and
you'll find yourself under a Ledge that contains a
Jar. Jump up—Mario and Toad will have a tough
time doing this—and use the Potion in the Grass to
the right of the Jar (there are Vegetables in the two
clumps to the left). You can now enter the Jar in
Subspace and warp to World Seven; the choice is
yours! (Halfway through this level, you may *wish*
you'd warped ahead.) If you stay here, continue
right. Just after the Palm Trees are three Grasses:
Potion on the left, two Vegetables on the right. Use
the Potion here, or bring it with you. Watching ou

for Albatosses above unleashing Bob-Ombs in your
direction—remember: these dudes kill by touch *or*
by exploding—move ahead, collecting Cherries.
When you reach the Hill, you'll find Grasses on top
with Potion (left) and Vegetables (all the rest).
Whether you use this Potion or carried the previous
Potion with you, be sure to use it at the foot of the
Hill in order to obtain a Mushroom. The next land-
mark you'll encounter is a T-shaped Log formation,
by which time you should have collected enough
Cherries to bring on Starman. If you haven't—
watch out! When you reach the Log Ledge in front
of the Towerlike Tree, you'll be besieged by Bob-
Ombs. You can plow through them if you're invincible; if not, take hip-hopping jumps to get over and
past them. There's a Vegetable in the Grass patch
on the Log (right side) if you need it, and another
Vegetable in the clump on the Log in front of the
next Tree Tower, just past the Hill. (Note: you don't
want to go on those Logs if you don't have to; it's
quicker to go under the first one, up onto the Hill,
then under the second one—a cinch if you have
Starman, but still do-able if you're just plain Luigi.)
A short plain follows the second Tree Tower, after which you'll reach a Wall with a Ledge above.
Go up. There are three Grasses: two Bob-Ombs with
a Potion in the center. Use the Bob-Ombs to blow
up the Wall—keeping in mind that they explode
much faster than ordinary Bombs, so there's no
time to tarry! When you've broken the Wall, use
the Potion and collect the Mushroom. Then pluck
the Grass to the right of the destroyed Wall to get

a normal Bomb and blow up the Wall to the right
This will allow you to access a Ladder—the onl
way out of this region. Upon descending, you'll fin
yourself in a corridor with a Jar to the right and
Mushroom Block on top of it. When you remove th
Block, Bob-Ombs will emerge. Hurry to the left an
when you reach the narrow Ledge at the end of th
corridor, grab one of the pursuing Bob-Ombs an
use it to destroy the Wall beneath the Ledge. (.
Shell in the lone Grass clump to the left of the Wa
will help deal with any other Bob-Ombs menacin
you.) Beyond the razed Wall you'll find Grasse
from the left they are a Bomb, four Vegetables, an
on the far right, Potion. Enter Subspace here t
reap the riches, then continue left. When you reac
the Pit, jump up to the Wall ahead—there's a Ve
etable in the Grass clump—cross the Log in front
the first Tree Tower (the Grass on the Log contai
a Vegetable), hop to the other Log, and enter th
door in the second Tree Tower. This new room's
corker! It's the inside of the Tree: a vertical chan
ber with passages exiting left and right in the u
per half. When you exit one, you reenter on th
other side of the room. That's handy, since you ha
foes like a walking Panser to deal with. (If yo
choose to stand and fight the Panser which attac
shortly after you arrive, there are Mushroom Bloc
to the right, immediately above where you ent
the chamber.) The only way to get to your goal, t
top of the chamber, is to go to the bottom and the
head up the left side. In addition to the Panse
you'll have Sparks to fight as well as a pair of Ja

that release Shyguys. There are Mushroom Blocks all over the place; throw them at the former, and use them to plug the Jars.

When you reach the top and pass through the door, you'll find yourself on a Log with Grasses to the right; there are Vegetables in all. The next two Logs contain nothing useful—which isn't the same as containing nothing at all: you have enemies here, remember! You'll need Pidgit's Carpet to cross the chasm beyond the last Log; pay no attention to the Pidgit that passes when you near the next Tree Tower. Hop onto the Log, the Grasses of which are all Vegetables. Proceed by hopping across the Clouds, then wait when you get to the first T-shaped Log edifice: there are three such structures in a row, and Birdo is on the last of them. Use the Eggs to make an omelette of the creep, then climb the Staircase beyond. Eliminating Birdo was only the first step in exiting World Five: in the next room, you've got to deal with Clawgrip. This crab digs into a pile of Rocks and throws them at you; your task is to grab them after they've landed and throw them back. Since you have to cross a narrow Pit, Rock in hand, this is one region where, conceivably, Toad would give you a *slight* advantage. However, his presence here is not worth having to suffer through the earlier stages with his meager abilities. When Clawgrip evaporates, you are ready to enter—

6/1: Well, T.E. Lawrence, here's just what you needed: more deserts, more unstable sands, and

more Cobrats. Actually, the challenge here is no
so much to survive—which is relatively easy—as t
find Key objects . . . if you get our meaning. To be
gin, travel to the first Jar. Kill the Cobrat, ente
the Jar, get Potion from the Grass, exit, and ente
Subspace atop the rib cage to the right of the Jar
When the Mushroom materializes, snatch it quickl
or it'll be swallowed up by the sands. Continue t
the right, dealing with old foes, until you reach th
two Jars: use the Shell found in the first to bop th
Cobrat that emerges from the second. Frankly, thi
part is pretty mundane; after the Jars, you'll cros
more desert, encountering the likes of Panser an
Pokey, as well as Grasses with a Vegetable and Po
tion, in that order; go right, use the Potion on to
of the golden hut at the end of the desert, and you'l
get a Mushroom. (In normal-space, the Grasse
there all contain Vegetables.) When you're done
enter the hut and go to the edge of the Ledge. Thi
is the fun part: there are 21 Jars before you. If yo
want to explore them all, go ahead. However, wha
you need is the Key buried in the sands of the fift
Jar from the right—you'll also find a 1-Up in th
third Jar from the left. With the Key, you'll be abl
to open the door in the right side of the room. Tha
will lead you to Birdo's chamber: the blue bird
unhappiness is only spitting fire and not chuckin
Eggs, but that also means you can't catch them an
throw them back. What you need to do is carry th
Mushroom Blocks, one at a time, to the top of th
Staircase and toss them onto the boss. There ar

only three Blocks, so don't miss, or you'll have to go down right next to Birdo to get them back.

6/2: Like 6/1, this is a short level—but fear not, 6/3 makes up for it. If you're not Luigi or the Princess, you're going to have to make a big jump to climb the second step of the Staircase in the first room. Accomplishing this and exiting, you'll be on a Ledge with one Grass (a Vegetable); the only way to get off is to ride an Albatoss. Once you're on board, soar over the Wall with the Panser and dismount when you reach the Wall with the Grasses. The Grass on the left has Potion—the right clump has a Vegetable. Enter Subspace here, then hitch a ride on a leftward-headed Albatoss—that's the only direction they'll be flying out here—and go back to the beginning. Mount an Albatoss flying to the right—only this time you won't have to get off on the Wall with the Potion. Shortly after you pass this point, a stack of Albatosses will come flying at you: it will be necessary to jump *over* the trio and land back on your Albatoss when it has flown through the flock. Leave your winged taxi when you reach the narrow Wall (the one with the Grass—a Vegetable) and hop to the Wall beyond. Pass through the door and you'll be in Birdo's chamber—we *told* you this realm was short! First, get the Mushroom Block from the ground and bring it to the Ledge directly above Birdo. Drop that one, and the one already up there, onto the big-nosed boss. Then go down, grab the handiest of those two Mushroom Blocks, and heave it at Birdo to conclude the battle.

6/3: Like we said before ... this region's a fa
one, full of danger and nifty sights. To begin with
when you get off the Ladder, do so on the *left* side
Let yourself sink into the sands, and you'll be o
the other side of that Wall to your left. Where wi
you end up? At a door that will take you to th
Pyramid at the end of 6/3! Should you care to battl
your way through, head right off the Ladder
There's Grass with Potion at your feet, but don
use it here: carry it to the second rib cage and ope
Subspace there. You'll find the Mushroom atop th
cactus. The only other thing you need to know abou
the desert is that there's a Bomb in the lone Gras
ahead, following the second rib cage after Sul
space; you won't need it for a Wall, so use it agains
your enemies. After entering the door in the ston
building, you'll have to play some heads-up vide
gaming. Bob-Ombs will start charging you from th
Jars, but don't panic. Grab the nearest Ladde
hang onto it, and wait until the walking explosive
detonate. (Be certain, though, that when you go u
the first Ladder, you collect the Cherries on eithe
side.) When they do, they'll take the nearest Ja
with them. Dig down at the right side of the fir
and second sandpits to get Cherries.

When you reach the sand Wall to the right—th
one standing there in defiance of the laws of gra
ity—dig to the right and then *up* to the top of th
stone Wall. Both Grasses contain Bombs. Take on
go back into the sand, use the explosive to make
hole at the bottom of the stone Wall on the righ

go back and get the second Bomb, make the hole larger, and go through. Get the Cherries on top of the sands in here; if you've gotten all the others in this room—and there's no reason you shouldn't have!—Starman will arrive. And a good thing, too: Ninji after Ninji will attack. Without invincibility, your chances of surviving are not good. Burrow up through the sands to the right, head right when you reach the stones, and pull the Grasses to get rid of the Wall in front of you. If you blew up the Wall so that a Pit was created, you can drop down— but make certain you skew Mario to the left or right, or he'll tumble to his death in the Pit below the first Pit. If you do this, however, you'll miss out on a Subspace encounter. So, instead of dropping down, go right. Skip the first Grass (the Potion) for now and get the second (a Bomb). Place the explosive at the Wall, blow it up, and ignore the next Grass (another Bomb). Take the Bomb from the Grass after that, however, and hurry down the Ladder to the right. Run to the left and use the Bomb to blow up the Wall. (All the Grasses you'll pass here are Vegetables.) If you need another Bomb, go back and get the one you skipped before—keeping in mind that it's a slightly longer distance to travel and the Bomb *may* explode before you arrive, blowing you to subatomic particles! Assuming you made it, go back now and get the Potion. Bring it down the Ladder and use it at the broken Wall; you'll have no trouble getting the Mushroom that appears. Upon emerging from Subspace, return to the Ladder. (Incidentally, while there *are* more rooms

to the left, you've no reason to go to them now
there's nothing in them but Grasses containin
Bombs and Vegetables.) Leave the Ladder whe
you've gone high enough to clear the Wall on th
right, then walk to the Vine. Climb.

You're now in a realm that boasts more Vine
than the Amazon! Climb up the right cliff an
when the Hoopsters are low down—they're inf
mously low-down, but that's another story!—h
onto the Vine on the left. When you reach th
Cloud, transfer to the left again. You'll see how
proceed from here, simply by looking at the way th
Vines are hanging; how you ascend also depen
upon where the Hoopsters are. However, here a
a few things to look out for. When you reach th
first long Cloud with a series of short Vines han
ing side by side, make the transfers by pushing bo
up and right or left on the control pad. You'll ru
into Shyguys and Snifits shortly after clearing th
abovementioned Vines. Watch the Snifits whe
they shoot, and note carefully just where their pr
jectiles go; position yourself right below that sp
and, during a lull in the firing, scoot past the ba
sters. The last real danger spot is several Clouds u
you'll see one Vine hanging down from the left, a
three from the right—they get successively short
the farther to the right they are. Do *not* go up tho
Vines on the right: the Hoopsters are truly dange
ous here. Stay to the left for the remainder of yo
ascent.

When you reach the top of the last Vine, head
the right and the golden Pyramid. (If you warp

ere from the beginning of this World, you'll be to he far right of the Pyramid, on a Cloud. To reach he Structure, make your way to the left, across the Clouds.) Inside the Pyramid you'll be battling Birdo. (Gee . . . what a surprise!) And while there's a Mushroom Block here, it's useless: you'll need to get on top of it in order to jump to the Ledge where Birdo is standing. So, just like in the old days, you'll have to fight the Egg-tossing, fire-breathing monster using the captured Eggs. Upon defeating Birdo, you'll be ushered into the presence of Tryclyde. Truth be told, the serpent isn't as tough as it looks. Take three Mushroom Blocks from the *right* side of he row of Blocks and stack them one atop the other n the Ledge in front of Tryclyde—erecting them in he center of the Ledge is fine. When you stand on op of these, you'll be taller than the dragon and ts flames won't touch you. Go back down to the row f Mushroom Blocks, pick one up, climb the Mushoom Block Wall you built, and toss the Block at Tryclyde. Do this with the remaining two Mushoom Blocks: score three direct hits and Tryclyde vill go bye, Clyde!

/1: This is it: Wart's Castle! The first part, 7/1, is oing to be comparatively short and easy . . . somehing that is *not* true of the last world in the game, /2. Upon arriving, you'll find yourself on a Cloud. Climb the Cloud steps to the Ladder, ascend, and ead right, ready to do battle with Albatosses, Bob-Ombs, and Ninjis. Above all, be sure that you *stay ahead of the Bob-Ombs*: when they explode, here,

they take sections of the stone Bridges with the
leaving nothing but the gaping holes and the eth
ahead of you! You can perch atop the Columns
avoid their blasts, if need be. After the first st
Bridge, you'll come to the Mushroom-shaped roo
a house. The Grasses there all contain Vegetabl
However, at the end of the next stone Bridge i
Column with Potion Grass on top; take it, go l
and work magic on the roof. Just do so with has
or the Bob-Ombs will waste you. Recross the st
Bridge to the right, hop onto the Cloud, use
Mushroom Block as a cork to plug up the Jar ahe
and enter the house ahead. Avoiding the Spa
inside, get onto the top Ledge and grab the th
Grass from the right: it's Potion! Enter Subsp
here and reap the Mushrooms and Coins. Exit a
get onto the roof, pulling the Vegetable there to I
any Shyguy who happens to be about. Then bo
an Albatoss for the long ride *left* . . . back to
beginning of the world. Go *past* the point where j
started your trek, continuing left until you re:
another Ladder. To the left of it is a Column, a
beyond that a single Grass; yank it and a Roc
will appear . . . your only ticket out of this secti

When you land, you'll be in a horizontal Cl-
region. Get the Cherries on the lower level, t
double back a few paces and get onto the up
Cloud. Hop the Column ahead, then the one at
that, and stop when you reach the next Colu:
Get the Cherries on top of the Column below
to the right, then fall in behind a Shyguy hea
toward the Cherries below, at the base of the C

mn: follow him and you'll reach the goodies un-
cathed. Get on top of the Column and head right
o the Ladder. Hop up three Clouds—watching out
or Sparks—and you'll find some Mushroom Blocks.
Jse these to bop Sparks, then stack them so you
an reach the next Ladder with ease. Climb and,
gain, use the Mushroom Blocks to kill Sparks,
hen arrange the Blocks so you can get to the Cloud
bove. Climb one of the two central Ladders to the
adder between them, then take either the Ladder
n the left or right to reach the hut. Enter for your
mpteenth battle with Birdo. Take the room's one
lushroom Block to the edge of Birdo's Ledge and
lobber the creature; reclaim the Mushroom Block
vhen you can and hit your foe two more times. The
ey to surviving here is to keep hopping to avoid
eing hit; don't hesitate to drop off the Ledge, if
eed be.

/2: You've now reached the Castle proper, and
hings're about to get pretty interesting . . . not to
aention long, arduous, and challenging! To begin,
o right along the Clouds and cross the drawbridge.
ross the thin catwalk inside, with an eye on the
hyguy Jar—you'll have to jump 'em; there are no
reapons here! After the Jar, you'll come to another
ain catwalk . . . only this and successive walks all
aove! If that weren't bad enough, you have to fight
'injis, Bob-Ombs, and Shyguys as you cross. Move
lowly but don't stop; a steady rightward movement
rill get you through. When you reach the sole float-
ag Block with a Chain hanging from it, you have

a choice: whether to go down here or to continue
the end of this room and take a different route
tirely. The two meet up eventually, but both o
different challenges. So that you can make an
formed choice, we'll look at both routes.

Route One: Climb down the Chain. You'll end
in a vertical chamber whose floors are made
tirely of Mushroom Blocks. Pick them up to g
yourself access to the floors below ... and also
keep the Sparks at bay. Make sure you get all
Cherries in the room. The door at the bottom
take you to a horizontal room filled with hang
Chains and killer Sparks. Use the Chains like
used the Ladders back in 6/3, as a place to hang
(literally) until your enemies wander off. There
two doors in this room: both take you to differ
places. (You didn't think Wart would live in
easy-to-negotiate Castle, did you?) However,
time you'll want to enter both. The first door ta
you to a secret chamber. The danger-free room
tains Potion; use it and exit by the same
through which you entered. You'll be back in
horizontal Chain room; continue to the right, a
watching out for Sparks. Enter the door in
room's far-right corner. Climb the Chain. Altho
the Chain will be broken in spots as you ascen
this vertical chamber, bridging the gaps is e
Indeed, there's nothing too difficult about this ro
if you stay on the Chain and don't veer slightl
either side, the Sparks won't touch you. If you
cide to go for any of the Cherries that line the w

lo so speedily because *then* the Sparks will go after
you!

The door at the top will lead you to a small, hor-
zontal chamber with Sparks and Chains. You'll
ave to move fast, when the coast is clear, to go up
he short Staircase to the left, past the second Chain
and onto the third Chain. If you tarry, the Sparks'll
get you. Climb the Chain to enter a large vertical
oom. Anything special here? You bet! Moving
loors, populated by Shyguys, Sparks, and Snifits.
Do *not* stay in one place for very long: the key to
succeeding here is to keep moving upward in small
eaps. Otherwise, you'll be overwhelmed. You
hould move straight up the center until you reach
he Ledge below the Icicles, then go right. Climb
teadily to the left until you reach the top of the
Wall on that side, then study the four Ledges to the
ight to time your move. Once you clear these, it
oesn't matter whether you go up to the left or
ight. The Chain overhead is your ticket out of
ere—and into the presence of the last Birdo. You
an battle the bird or you can pass it—under or
ver—when it moves. Go up the Chain and head
ight at the top, past the Sparks, past the locked
oor, to the door beyond. Enter, and you'll find
ourself where you *would* have been had you
aken—

Route Two: Instead of climbing down the Chain,
o right across the Catwalks to the Chain at the
nd of the room. When you reach the next room, go
eft and shimmy up the Chain that leads through
he roof. (There's a room to the left, but don't worry

about that right now.) You're now in the bottom
a large vertical chamber which is comprised of
small rooms on the bottom and one large one ab
you must negotiate them using Chains and Ledg
The Sparks in the lower two rooms of this sect
won't trouble you much—treat them as you did
Hoopsters on the Vines earlier, timing your s
from Chain to Chain when the Sparks aren't ne
though the ones hovering around the first of
blue Ledges requires a bit of patience: you mus
for the Chain on the left (there's a door you'll w
to enter), so wait until the coast is clear, then r
ahead. Enter the door on the Ledge and you'll
yourself outside the Castle. Climb down the se
of Ladders, pausing when necessary to avoid I
ser's fire, or actually jumping off the Ladder
falling down the right side, along the wall of
Castle. Go into the door at the foot of the last I
der, and you'll find yourself in that room we n
tioned earlier. Get Potion from the Grass on
right, enter Subspace, collect the Mushroom,
head back through the door, up the Ladders,
back into the Castle. When you've returned to
vertical chamber with the Chains and Ledges,
tinue upward. One place to watch out for: the
small Columns sitting on the last Ledge. Spa
doggedly orbit that region as well as the Colt
and Ledge to the lower left. Once you commi
going through, do so *without stopping*, or yo
doomed. Climb the last Chain to the door on
upper right. Be alert as you enter the door: t
are Sparks galore on the other side. Use the Ch

for sanctuary and the POW for offense, then head right. When you've climbed the next Chain, you'll be on a long Catwalk. Climb down the Chain at the end, descend using the Chain at the right, and you'll find yourself in a small room with a door. This is the same place you'd have ended up if you'd taken *Route One*.) Enter, get the Key, and go to the locked door mentioned in *Route One*. Use the Key to enter. There are just two more rooms to clear.

The first room is a surprise: there *seems* to be no enemy here. However, when you near the Mask Door at the end, it won't open as usual: it will come off the wall and attack! Using the two Mushroom Blocks, score a total of three hits against the Mask and it will go back to where it belongs. Get the Crystal Ball and enter Wart's chamber. The big boss himself is sitting on the far-right side. He'll spit deadly Bubbles at you, while the Dream Machine in front of him ejects Vegetables. Your task: to catch the Vegetables and hit Wart when his mouth is open—but before he blows Bubbles. That's the only time he's vulnerable. When the chief villain has been fatally weakened, he'll change colors and expire.

And that frees Mario for his most complex and exciting adventure yet!

SUPER MARIO BROS. 3

jective:

Looks like there's never going to be a moment's rest for Mario. Bowser's back, intent on conquering the Mushroom World ... the realm beyond the Mushroom Kingdom. And *this* time Bowser's brought his putrid progeny, just to make things really unnerving. Specifically, the evildoers have stolen the Magic Wands from each nation of the Mushroom World and used them to transform each of the kings into beasts. (What? No queens? An enlightened place like the Mushroom World should *not* be chauvinistic!) Needless to say, Mario—or the Princess, Luigi, or Toad—must dare new dangers to defeat the villains and restore normalcy to the world.

Gameplay:

The most important innovations are the new pow
that Mario et al. can acquire. By catching a pow
up, Mario can become Raccoon Mario, able to
and whack enemies with his tail. A Fire Flow
transforms Mario into Fire Mario, able to thr
fireballs. You also become Frog Mario during
course of the game and when surrounded by fc
can briefly become invincible—albeit immobil
Statue Mario if you're already Raccoon Ma
There are also the familiar Coins, Starman, 1-
Mushrooms, and Super Mushrooms to acquire.
for the Blocks, there are Jump Blocks, ? Blocks
before, and Switch Blocks marked with a P wh
cause unpredictable results when touched. Otl
additions to the line-up include Toad's House, wh
allows Mario to pick up important tools, and
Spade Panel, in which additional Marios
awarded to players who correctly match rolling p
tions of a picture. Other items, such as Juger
Cloud and Magic Wing, will be discussed where
propriate. The enemy characters are pictured
described in the instruction booklet, and will
mentioned in the *Strategies* section below as t
crop up.

Points:

Points are awarded for virtually everything Ma
does, from defeating enemies to collecting Coins
power-ups: 50 points for a Coin, 100 for boppin
Para-Goomba, and 1000 for nabbing a power-

Bosses must be clobbered a number of times; each time you do so, the point value doubles; that is, 1000, 2000, 4000.

ategies:

First, some general tips. When you go to one of the special screens containing one or more Hammer Brothers—or their Boomerang, etc., kin—you can stand right next to them and not be hurt: their weapons will arc over you. To destroy them, wait until they go back onto the Blocks, then get underneath and bop them off. Make sure that you hit all the Blocks for additional goodies.

As for the Spade rooms, they all follow one of these patterns. After you've turned over one Card, you'll know what to expect next by referring to the chart below:

1. Top Row: Mushroom, Flower, 20 Coins, Mushroom, Ten Coins, Star
   Middle: Flower, 1-Up, Mushroom, Ten Coins, 1-Up, 20 Coins
   Bottom: Star, Flower, Star, Mushroom, Flower, Star
2. Top: Flower, Star, 1-Up, Flower, 1-Up, Mushroom
   Middle: Ten Coins, Mushroom, Flower, Star, Mushroom, Ten Coins
   Bottom: Star, 20 Coins, 20 Coins, Mushroom, Flower, Star
3. Top: Flower, Star, 1-Up, Flower, 1-Up, Mushroom

Middle: Ten Coins, Mushroom, Flower, Star, Mushroom, Ten Coins

Bottom: Star, 20 Coins, 20 Coins, Mushroom, Flower, Star.

4. Top: Flower, Ten Coins, 1-Up, Flower, 1-Up, Mushroom

Middle: Star, Mushroom, 20 Coins, Star, Mushroom, Ten Coins

Bottom: Star, Flower, 20 Coins, Mushroom, Flower, Star

5. Top: Mushroom, Flower, 1-Up, Flower, Star, Star

Middle: 20 Coins, Star, Mushroom, Ten Coins, 1-Up, Flower

Bottom: 20 Coins, Mushroom, Ten Coins, Mushroom, Flower, Star

6. Top: Mushroom, Flower, 20 Coins, Flower, Ten Coins, Star

Middle: 20 Coins, 1-Up, Mushroom, Ten Coins, 1-Up, Flower

Bottom: Star, Mushroom, Star, Mushroom, Flower, Star

7. Top: 1-Up, Mushroom, Ten Coins, Mushroom, Flower, Star

Middle: Mushroom, Ten Coins, Star, 20 Coins, 20 Coins, Flower

Bottom: Star, 1-Up, Flower, Mushroom, Flower, Star

8. Top: Flower, 20 Coins, Mushroom, Star, 1-Up, Flower

Middle: 1-Up, Flower, Ten Coins, Mushroom, 2

Coins, Star
Bottom: Mushroom, Ten Coins, Star, Mushroom, Flower, Star

Now . . . let's boogie!

rass Land

1/1: World One is going to be a cinch for experienced Marioers. Scroll the screen left as little as possible until you've gotten the Mushroom from the fourth? (the other ?'s are Coins). The first Pipe contains a fireball-spitting Venus Fire Trap; leap over it between the blasts and hunker down on the right side of the pipe. The plant can't get you there. (When you get good, you can actually leap over the Venus Fire Trap and get past it before it can fire!) Continue right, hopping over the green and orange Walls, killing the Turtlelike Koopa by leaping on it from the left—and hopping back to the left after you bash it. Kick the Shell into the next ? to release the power-up, and go collect it before it falls off the bottom of the screen. Get the Coin from the ? then prepare to deal with the Goombas and a Para-Goomba—which has wings and must be bopped twice—on the long stretch just ahead. Clobber them all, then head back to the left—to the power-up Block—accelerate, and take to the skies flying diagonally to the upper right, following the string of Coins and, natch, collecting them all. (For beginners, it's best to build up speed thusly. Put the con-

troller on a flat surface. With one hand, hold th
pad down and keep the B button pressed in, whi
with the other hand push the A button.) On th
first set of Jugem's Clouds, bump the glowing Bloc
overhead, then scoot up on the right side of th
Block to collect the Mushroom. Continue righ
gathering all the Coins, then do *not* descend; fly
the right until you reach the Pipe, and go down.
will take you to a Coin room. When you emerg
you'll be just a few hops from the end of the level. (
you didn't enter the Pipe but dropped down, you
land on a stack of glowing Blocks: bop the Koo
and use the Shell to smash them. You'll uncover
Switch Block here—top right of the bunch on th
left. By the way: as in other Mario games, ma
sure you don't get nailed if the Shell hits an i
passe and rebounds!) If possible, try to freeze th
timer at the end of the round with the clock sho
ing an even number and the Coin and point cou
each being a multiple of eleven.

1/2: The first ? in the new realm contains a powe
up, just in case you got demoted from Super Mari
Even if you didn't, get it: it's worth 1000 point
Watch out for the Para-Goombas after the Pip
Now, this part's important. Go to the right side
the T-shaped Pipe. Goombas will begin pouring ou
If you can crush nine of them, *without* touching th
ground, you'll get a 1-Up—plus all the points y
accumulated for mashing the little guys. Kee
stomping Goombas after that: you'll get an ad
tional 1-Up for *every one you bop!* Stay here as lo

as you want, collecting 1-Ups. When you continue to the right and reach the floating Coins with the Pipe and Venus Fire Trap, collect the Coins only if you can fly. Otherwise, don't. Go past them, to the right, and hit the left Block of the Ledge *closest* to the ground, underneath the Pipe. It's a Switch Block and will turn the Coins to Blocks. You can use the Blocks to climb to the pipe, get a 1-Up Mushroom above and to the right of it, then slide down the Pipe and enter a Coin room. Even better, when you emerge you'll be at the Pipe *before* the one you entered, allowing you to collect the Coins now instead of turning them into Blocks. A few easy-to-beat Goomba-types will attack, after which you'll reach a pair of Jump Blocks; there's a power-up in the one on the right. Continue to the next Pipe, sliding down the hill and crouching on the left side of the Pipe—to avoid the Venus Fire Trap. When the plant retreats, hop over and continue: you'll run into three Jump Blocks, the third of which contains a Starman. The last ? is a Coin; the end of the round is just beyond.

1/3: Stomp the first Koopa you see, pick up its Shell, and sling it at the next foe that attacks you; the Shell will continue beyond and smash a few of the Blocks ahead. When you arrive, squash the red Koopa and use its Shell to obliterate the Blocks; when you've cleared a path so you can stand at the right of the ? (which contains a power-up), leap straight up. You'll uncover an invisible Jump Block. Hop on and it'll vault you into the stratosphere. There, you can collect mucho Coins and 1-Up Mushroom without an enemy in sight! De scend the Pipe and you'll be deposited at the end the level. If you decided to stay on the ground, yo can collect Coins there—though not nearly as man as above. However, there *is* one enormous benef to staying on the ground. If you stand on the whit Wall above the foliage—the third Block from th left—and squat in the center, you'll fall *through* th Wall and end up in a hidden Toad House wher you'll find a Magic Whistle. If you blow it now, yo can warp ahead to World Two, Three, or Four. It better, however, to save it and use it when you'v found the other Whistles.

1/4: This is a realm of Ledges and floating Logs. B careful when you use the latter: they're extremel useful, but dangerous in that they drift over an then drop suddenly. Make sure you're not on when it does so, or it's kaput time! After you leav the *third* Log, you'll come to a short Ledge with smaller one beneath it, the two of them flush o the right. If you're good, you can jump up agains the upper Ledge from the Log. If you're still lear ing the ropes, get on the lower Ledge, jump u against the upper Ledge, and you'll uncover Mushroom in the second Block from the right. Gra it quickly, or it'll fall away. Continue to the righ hit the leftmost Block of the Ledge that has prowling Koopa—the fiend is red—and you'll ge multiple Coins. Bop Koopa—or, if you time it righ you can slay the Turtle simply by hitting up on th

Coin Block when the creature is just to the right of it—pick up its Shell, ride the next Log, and throw the Shell against the lone Block standing on the right of the Ledge on top. You'll get another Mushroom. When you come to the vertical string of Coins, hop on the Log and ride it down to collect them ... jumping off to the right, onto the *top* of the L-shaped Ledge. Jump up against the Block above and you'll get multiple Coins. You'll reach a Pipe in a few moments, and it'll take you to the end of the level. You'll be able to play match the cards now: do a good job and you can get five extra Marios! Note: if you accumulate at least 44 Coins in this level, you'll be allowed to enter the White House on the map screen. There, you'll be able to acquire a P-Wing.

World One Fortress: after leaping three pits, hit the first ? for a power-up. When you enter the corridor ahead, wafflelike foes called Rotodiscs will attack from the ceiling. These move in a clockwise direction—except for the first, which orbits counterclockwise. If you're Raccoon Mario, fly over these foes altogether; if not, after you get through the corridor and leap three pits, make sure you hit the next ? for a power-up. Immediately after the ? you'll encounter Dry Bones for the first time. Right after you beat the mummified Turtle, go to the far right *without* entering the door. Hold down the B button and accelerate, running to the left: fly up, go over the Wall (heading right) and continue traveling right, along the top of the Wall, until you reach a room. There, you'll find the second Whistle, which

you should add to your arsenal instead of using
Go to the map and continue your quest. If you did
take this route, then after you kill Dry Bones, en
the door beyond the dusty tortoise, and the ceili
will come down to crush you. No problem—as lc
as you make sure that when it does, you snug
into one of the little alcoves in the ceiling. Ev
though there are Spikes in these, you'll be sa
(Note: if you rush ahead when the ceiling starts
descend, you'll be able to reach the second—a
last—alcove in one spring. You *can* make it, a
you'll be in an ideal position to enter the next d
when the ceiling rises.) That next door takes you
the mini-boss Boom Boom; as soon as you spot h
run over, jump on the creature's head three tim
and it's bye bye Boom Boom.

1/5: This is an ice realm, and you begin by slid
down an incline and demolishing the Buzzy Beet
waiting for you. After you somersault over the P
collecting the Coins as you go—watch out for
downward-facing Pipe: a deadly plant waits with
Once past this, you can go one of two ways: al
the upper corridor, or to the right of the Pipe bel
If you take the high road, you'll find an invisi
Jump Block at the top left of the corridor. Leap
it and you'll be catapulted to Clouds filled w
Coins. Make sure that you fly *over* the layer of Co
close to the Clouds: there's another level higher
along with a Block containing a 1-Up Mushro
The Pipe will return you to the surface more th
halfway through the realm. If you took the l

:oad, watch out for the killer plant in the first Tube.
Beyond it, you'll find Coins—jump in the water and
hop up and down to get the moolah—and, at the end
before the corridor slopes up), you'll get a Flower
Írom the ?. You'll emerge at the same place from
which the Pipe would've dropped you if you'd gone
.nto the Clouds. Climb the ice steps, slide down the
slope, nail the Koopa, then go down the Pit *carefully* or you'll slip right into the waiting maw of
.he Venus Fire Trap that lives in the first Pipe.
You can also use the slain Koopa to bop the
Flower.) The first downward-facing Pipe also con-
,ains a deadly plant. When you get past it and re-
•merge on the surface, the round will be over. (Note:
f you start running just to the left of the jagged
ine that separates the sky from the black, and jump
ıt the Card, you'll almost always get a Star.)

1/6: There's an interesting new gadget on this level:
Logs that ride along on wire tracks, colloquially
known as Rail Lifts. When you begin, a Koopa first
appears on the Log with the floating Coins. Bop it
and toss its Shell down to the right to destroy the
Koopa on the Log below. Get the power-up from the
? above that Log. Continue right: you'll pass a green
hub atop a Log, two Jump Blocks, a green Hill on
a Log beyond them and, a bit farther, a green Hill
vith two small vertical Walls of Blocks and a Ledge
above it—as well as a Koopa between them. Kill the
Koopa, use its Shell to bash its winged companion
o the left, then bust up the Blocks overhead: the
second Block from the right contains a 1-Up Mush-

room. Hop on the first Log suspended by blue
bles; at the end, get on the skinny Log and st
running, continuing across the next cable-suppor
Log: it's difficult, but you should be able to
enough speed going to fly up to get the float
Coins. If not, drop down to the sole Block at the
of the first cable-supported Log and get on the w
guided Log to the right. The former tack, obviou
will get you more Coins. If you are able to fly,
low the Coins downward until you land on the I
below the last group. The wire-pulled Log will le
you off here as well. (If you take the wire-dri
Log, watch out for the winged Turtle that will d
down on you.) From here, it's an easy few hops
the end of the level. (Beware: there's a Koopa w
ing for you beneath the Card! Be sure you jum
little earlier than usual.)

World One Ship: it's time to do battle on the f
of the Koopa Ships you'll encounter. First, thou
congrats to the programmer who came up with
ominous drumbeat that opens this round. It's
per! Before you begin, here's a sorry bit of ne
your fireballs are useless on the boat. Speed
agility are your primary "weapons." Howev
they're not your only weapon: if you stand on
top of a cannon, your feet just overhanging
mouth, the Bullet Bills that come out won't h
you *and* you'll get 100 points for each one you s
in this fashion. To begin your crossing, no soo
do you board the ship than Cannons begin firin
you. Pass the first one and stand directly behin
until the second one has fired, then run ahead

get behind—to the right of—that one. Duck: a third Cannon, firing horizontally instead of diagonally like the first two, will take Mario's head off if you don't! What's more, this Cannon fires in both directions, so *don't* stand behind it; instead, jump down to the next platform—you can't miss it: there's another diagonally-firing Cannon to the right—and hug the Wall on the left. When the diagonally-firing Cannon has fired, jump it and continue to the right. Cross that small Wall quickly: not only will the horizontally-firing Cannon be shooting, still, but there's a diagonally-shooting Cannon in the upper right firing down at that very Wall. Cross the deck to the next thin Wall—with a horizontally-shooting Cannon on it. There's a diagonally-shooting Cannon above it to the right; hop on the Cannon on the Wall when it and the one above have just fired. When you're on the other side, you're safe until you reach the ? Block. There's a Flower in there, and you should get it . . . but don't dally. Above, to the right, is a Cannon that not only fires in *four* directions, it rotates to make sure one gun is always trained on you! Hop the Wall in front of you and push ahead, and you'll be safe. After a short section of deck, you'll see another diagonally-shooting Cannon aimed to the upper right. Slip into the alcove behind it. When the Cannon has fired, hop over it and run forward. The horizontally-firing Cannon in front of you won't touch you if you stay on the ground. Hop it and hug the right side of the Wall it's on; when it and the diagonally-shooting Cannon to its right have fired, rush up the Staircase. (You can leap the Wall and run up the steps in one broken sprint ... but that's only advised for ex rienced players.) Enter the Pipe on the top of Staircase and you'll do battle with the first of B ser's kids: Larry. He'll throw Smoke Rings at y but these are easy to dodge. All you have to d jump on his head three times—when he's out of Shell—and he's a goner. The Wand is yours, one king has been restored!

Desert Land

2/1: Upon entering this arid, sandy world, get der the first ? Block and wait. You'll be faced v hopping Blocks known as Pile Driver Mi Goombas on this level. These are apparently st Blocks that suddenly leap at you from the side Block will hop at you from the right; when it's r above the ? Block, jump up and hit the ? Th release a power-up *and* smash the incoming Mi Goomba. There's another Micro-Goomba just to right of where the last one took off—the top B at the end of the next section of Blocks—so jum it before it can launch itself. You'll find nothin any Blocks until you reach the small two-Block izontal Ledge of ?'s after the three vertical W (Note: there are Micros atop each Wall, so fly if you're Raccoon Mario.) The rightmost ? cont a Starman. Bash the Koopa below and, if missed the Starman, use the Turtle's Shell to sm the Micro to the right. Beware the Fire Snake

before the third Micro—which, when smashed, will
give you a power-up. Use the Jumping Blocks that
follow and vault up to the "runway" ahead. Kill
the Goombas, then drop off the right side of the
runway, bop the Block on the left, collect the power-
up, hit the empty space to the right of that Block
to uncover an invisible Jumping Block, then go left,
under the runway, and break the underside. Go inside and collect the Coins and a Mushroom from the
lone Block. (You can avoid the Fire Snake in there
by bopping the Block, then tucking yourself into
the left corner below it and wait for the Mushroom
to reach you. The snake can't get you here.) Hop
onto the Ledge to the left, break through the runway to the top, go right to the edge, then run left
and fly up to the floating Pipe, which you can enter
by shattering the Blocks around it with your tail.
The Switch Block inside will reveal a load of Coins.
When you drop from the Coin room, you'll be on
another runway with Blocks and a Fire Snake inside. Break the last Block on the top, run to the
right to the next Pipe, then run back and the Blocks
will all be Coins. Break in using the Block on the
lower right, wait patiently for the Fire Snake to
come out, jump in and collect the Coins, then exit
using the Block on the upper left—that way, the
Fire Snake won't get you. Return to the Pipe on
the right, go to the one beyond it, and enter when
the killer Flower descends. (It's also suggested that
you return to the Pipe up above: you can collect the
Coins all over again!) After doing the Switch Block

routine and clearing the Coins from this room, y
will have completed the level.

2/2: This level will gift you with a visit to the Wh
Mushroom House if you collect at least 30 Coi
That *includes* all the Blocks that can become Co
when you use the Switch Block. To begin: bop t
Goomba, get past the killer plant, and hit the fi
Block for a power-up. There's another plant af
the pipe, and a sea after the first Wall. If you've
Raccoon power, you can ride the Log and then
if not, you'll have to go for a dip at some point. F
ing, you'll be dealing with your winged Turtle pa
swimming, it's killer fish whose touch is deadly.
cidentally—if you're good, you can stay in the
even if you're not Raccoonized. Simply bounce
the backs of the airborne Koopas as you go alo
Anyway—go through the level and collect all t
visible Coins, then go back to the left and get on t
Log. As you cross the lake again, hit the right Bl
of the first Ledge; it's a Switch Block. Quic
gather all the Coins that were Blocks so you can
to the White Mushroom room. The Pipe at the e
takes you out of this level and to—

World Two Fortress: your new foes here are t
Thwomps, big ugly-faced Blocks that crush wh
ever gets beneath them, rise, then get set to co
down again. These granite guys cannot be stopp
or destroyed. However, when they come down, y
can jump on top of and over them. The first appe
right after the initial trio of mummy Turtles. If y
keep stomping these Dry Bones as you did the Goo

bas in 1/2—that is, without touching the ground—
you can earn more 1-Ups as before. The second
Thwomp comes after the next herd of Turtles—
Turtle herdle? Immediately after you face the second Thwomp, the first Boo Diddly appears in the
upper left corner. You can wait until it comes down
low enough for you to jump on it, or simply race
ahead, bopping the Dry Bones as you pass. Enter
the Pipe at the far side of the room. When you
emerge, you'll have to cross a Spike Pit; no problem, you say—except that there's a Thwomp ready
to fall on the landing in the middle of the Pit. You
can make it across, though, if you race ahead without pausing on that Ledge. When you reach the
other side of the Spikes, hit the right Block of the
Ledge—below the second Boo Diddly: you'll get a
power-up. Then race like the wind to get past the
four Thwomps that fall in quick succession. You
can get through using a stop-and-go technique, but
there's no reason for caution here when speed will
do the trick! Enter the door at the end and you'll
be in a room whose Ledges are lined with Spikes
and come down toward the floor. These are best
taken using stop-and-go. Just don't stop anywhere
for *too* long, or the Boo Diddlies will come down and
get you. Upon entering the last chamber, you've got
to battle the Boom Boom Koopa. Jump on its head
three times to destroy it; just don't do so when its
porcupinelike quills are extended, or you'll perish.

2/3: Welcoming you to the next level is a Fire
Snake. Just go to the right until it scrolls off the

screen, then return to the left and it'll be gone. G
rid of the Koopa on the Pyramid and use its She
to break the Block beneath the ? on the right. The
get under the ? Block and hit it for a power-up. Th
next Pyramid has a Starman in the ? on the righ
The third Pyramid will give you a power-up—a S
per Leaf if you got the Mushroom at the first Py
amid—in the left ? Block. Beware the Micro at
the next Pyramid, and those jumping over from th
twin Pyramid beside it. Go to the Block to the le
of the Pyramid on the right, and hop up to the rig
using the two Jump Blocks. These will take you
a Ledge; fly from it to the upper left and you'll fir
two small Ledges, one atop the other. The upp
Ledge contains a Switch Block, which will turn th
Pyramids below into a slew of Coins! Droppir
down and collecting them, you'll have no troub
getting the 1-Up in the middle of the left Pyrami
If you can't get up to the Switch Block for son
reason, kill the Koopas here and use their Shells
smash the Pyramid on the left; fifth row from th
bottom, second Block from the right, contains th
1-Up Mushroom. The next (and last) structure
really a half Pyramid. When you arrive, smack a
the Blocks that comprise the Staircase on the le
you'll get a Coin from each. Then go to the edge
the top step, overlooking the Pit on the right. Jun
on top of one Koopa, then hop back up to the ste
pronto. Toss the Shell down and it'll smash th
Blocks covering the Pipe. Before you enter the Pip

get under the Block to the left, equal with the opening: hit it for multiple Coins.

World Two Desert: this is a relatively simple realm. After you pass the Venus Fire Traps, grab the Shell of the first Koopa you meet and carry it with you. When you meet the Whirlwind, jump right into its eye and let it cart you ahead. When you emerge, the Sun will try to set on you, chasing you around and giving new meaning to the word "sunburn." To protect yourself, use the Koopa Shell to smash the stellar pain in the neck.

2/4: To get the first ? Block, kill one of the Koopas—on the left or right Wall—and ricochet the Shell down against the ? Block. Jump down and claim the power-up. A little farther along is another Koopa: bop it and use the Shell to smack open the next ? and get another power-up. You should certainly have Raccoon Mario by now, which is important: most of the goodies in this level are located above. More on that in a moment. A Boomerang Brother is ahead, and in case you've been hit there's another power-up in the next ? Block—to the left of the Pipe with the killer Plant. When you reach the jagged line of demarcation at the end of the level, turn and fly to the *left*, following the Jumping Blocks—the lowest of which has a power-up. When you've reached the land in the sky, hit the second Block to the upper left to uncover a Switch Block. When you've gotten the Coins, go all the way to the lake on the left: stay on the right side of the Ledge above the water and hit the third Block from

the left—another Switch Block is here. Collect the
Coins, then head back to the right and exit ... but
watch it! A Boomerang Brother is waiting for you
below the Card. (Note: if you can get to the Card
before he throws, you'll be rewarded with a Coin
and 1000 points when the killer evaporates!) However, the most important thing to remember about
this level is none of the above! What's important?
The fact that you can get the third Magic Whistle
after winning here ... and, having gotten it, you
can use the three Whistles to warp to World Eight.
Go and battle the Hammer Brother wandering near
here, beat him, get the Hammer, and return to the
Map. Using the weapon, you can continue to the
right—even though the Map *seems* to end—where
you'll do battle with another Turtle; one of the Fire
Brothers. Kill him, and you'll get the last Whistle.
Now, use the Whistles to their limit! Obviously,
there is *one* serious disadvantage to taking a short
cut like this. You won't have the weapon you'll need
to make a dent in World Eight. Still, there's no
sense being faint-hearted: give it a try!

2/5: It's new foe time. This level introduces Chain
Chomp, the carnivorous ball-and-chain. Beware:
though the monster is fettered, the chain will break
after 160 timer-seconds have passed. So don't stand
around staring at the creature. Get the power-up in
the ? on the right only when the Chain Chomp is
chomping in another direction ... or slay it using
the Shell of the Koopa roaming to the right. The
next power-up is just beyond Chain Chomp number

two, in the Block on the ground, to the right of the Chomp's Block. You can snuggle under the Ledge to the right to get it, or kick it from the left when the Chomp is at rest. But hop on the Block quickly after you kick it, or the power-up will float away. As you cross the Wall to the right, you'll pass a water Pit and, after that, two Koopas: kill the one on top and throw its Shell against the sole Block to the right, beside a section of Wall, for a Coin. Now, just beyond that is a narrow Pit with a Ledge to the right and a second Pit beyond it. Bop the Koopa to the right of the second Pit, and carry the Shell back to the Pit on the left—the one just below the section of Wall where you got the Coin. It'll start smashing Blocks; when it hits the lowest Block on the left, a Vine will sprout. Climb it for floating Coins hidden above the Clouds, then enter the Pipe on the left side of this Coin heaven. Upon descending, bop the Block on the bottom right for a power-up, then hit the block directly *above* the one Block on the bottom, center. This is a Switch Block, and will turn all the Blocks to Coins. When you emerge from the Pipe, you'll be on a Wall in the sky: all of the ? Blocks contain Coins, save for the last one on the right, which will give you a power-up. Descend and exit the level. Since there are no foes under the Card, you can take a running leap at it to get a Star.

World Two Pyramid: this is a good place to be if you're just plain ol' Mario. If you enter the Pyramid, get a power-up, exit, and reenter: you can get the power-up again. The object in question is lo-

cated in the overhanging Block of the first Wall yo
encounter. Just bash the two Buzzies that get i
your way, slide down the ramp, and jump up to th
Ledge on your right. Smash the Wall up ahead
you, go past the Pipe with the Venus Fire Trap i
side, and head up to the Ledge on the left. Go le
At the Wall, jump up to the right. Shatter the Wa
ahead of you, pass under the Ledge, jump up to th
right of the Wall to uncover an Invisible Block, the
get on it and leap over the Wall so you can ent
the Pipe. Taking care not to shatter any Blocks u
less it's necessary, collect the Coins, get the 1-U
by jumping at the fifth Block from the right, on to
Then hit the lone Block on the bottom. Activate th
Switch Block to turn the remaining Blocks in
Coins. When you leave, you'll emerge from the Pi
to find a pair of Buzzies sliding down at you fro
the left. Run quickly up the slope on the right, the
continue right, along the corridor . . . watching o
for the Buzzies, who not only attack on the groun
but also crawl along the ceiling and drop down
you! Fortunately, you can use their Shells to bow
down others and to smack apart the Wall up ahea
Watch out for the killer plant in the Pipe just b
fore the Exit Pipe, and be prepared to battle th
Boomerang Brother who will be waiting for you
soon as you leave the Pipe—not below the Cards,
in most previous rounds.

World Two Ship: the not-so-warm welcome her
consists of two Cannons firing at you, one low ar
one high; they fire in reverse as well, so don't thir
you'll be safe by simply hopping over the first. Y

must get on top of the taller one and go from there to the upper deck. Naturally, things aren't going to be much fun up there; you'll take just a few steps and find yourself assaulted by a Cannon mounted on the side of the deck, firing diagonally to the upper right. That's easy enough to scoot past, but don't get overly confident: when you reach the end of the deck, make sure you drop down on top of the horizontally-firing Cannon down there, which hasn't quite scrolled onto the screen from the right yet—just jump as if it were there, and it'll scroll under you. If you land on the deck proper, that Cannon will perforate you. Leap off that Cannon to the Cannon on the deck below, to the right. Get off of it to the right, and hurry to the low Cannon there between shots. When you hop up to the deck on the right, make sure you do so immediately after a Bullet Bill has already come at you from the left. The ? on the new deck contains a Flower.

Jump down to the Crates and drop down the first gap between them, to the right, then head to the right—not the left, where the Cannons are. Waiting until a volley of Bullet Bills passes you by, drop down to the deck along the left side of the Mast. Negotiate this little zig zag course *without stopping*, or the Cannons will blast you to pulsating little particles. Hurry under the Mast and get on the Crate to its right. Go to the top of the Crates *fast* or the Cannons on the right will end your seafaring days. Continue along the Crate tops to the next deck on the right. Bop the "lids" of the Rocky Wrenches before they can rise from the deck and

throw Wrenches at you, then jump on top of t‖
second of the two Cannons ahead—like the one b‖
fore, it's the taller of the two. If you get on the fir‖
one, the second will kill you. Enter the Pipe beyo‖
to battle Morton Koopa Jr. Wait until he goes in‖
the little Pit beside his perch, then jump on hi‖
once. Go to the right—to his perch—and circle hi‖
clockwise when he jumps up at you, dropping dov‖
on his head when you're at the twelve o'clock p‖
sition. Repeat the orbit and hit him one more tim‖
three strikes and he's out. However, he's only vu‖
nerable when he's outside of his Shell.

Water Land

3/1: It's bathing suit time, folks. Drop into the w‖
ter and go straight down: you'll get a power-up‖
the ? under the big Sea Ledge. Swim left and u‖
then head right. You'll pass four upward-faci‖
Pipes and will eventually reach a set of ?'s with‖
Flower on the left and a Coin on the right. Whe‖
the Lava Lotus is still, pass under them from t‖
left to right, bopping both. Then go back to the le‖
to collect the Flower. Go up to the right of the Pi‖
overhead. Swim to the top of the water and use yo‖
jumping power to get on top of the Wall on the le‖
Cross to the left, drop into the little Pond up ther‖
and collect the power-up from the ? Retrace yo‖
steps to the right and dive back into the sea. Swi‖
over the three stalks of coral, then dive down to t‖
section filled with Jump Blocks. Beyond them,

the right, is a Block with a 1-Up Mushroom, surrounded by Coins. Be careful when you dogpaddle
up under the Block and bop it: if you're not quick,
the Mushroom will scurry away and fall, irretriev-
ably, into the Pit below. When you've got it, go to
the Pipe on the right and ride the current up to the
downward-facing Pipe above. Exit the level.

3/2: It's more Rail Lifts to start, though they move
faster than their predecessors. After you cross the
first two Rail Lifts—you can actually skip the second one by leaping over it—you'll reach a row of
Blocks (a Donut Lift) with a ? on the right. Just
stand on the Blocks and they'll fall, enabling you
to get under the ? for a Flower. Ride the next Rail
Log, shooting the leaping Cheep-Cheeps below
you—or jumping up and landing on them if you
don't have fireball power. Almost at once you'll be
passing under a Ledge with a lone Block on the left
side: get off and make absolutely certain that you
get the Starman in that Block. Not only will you become invincible, but there's a surprise, which we'll
tell you about in a second. Pass under the next ?
while riding the Rail Lift, and knock the Coins from
it. Now, when you pass under the next ?, you'll get
Coins . . . *unless* you got the Starman. If you did,
then you'll get another Starman here . . . and a
third Starman from the next ? you encounter, immediately after leaving the Lift. (If you didn't get
the first Starman, then the new ? will just be Coins
too.) Get on the second Rail Lift; while you travel
as before, watch out for the winged Koopa that de-

scends. (Note: don't use its Shell to shatter th
Blocks ahead. You'll want the Blocks intact!) Whe
you pass under the Ledge, hit the third Block fro
the left: it's a Switch Block. Beyond it, to the le
of the Pipe, is an Invisible Block that contains
1-Up. When you reach the Pipe, blast the plant insid
and go to the right, hop in the water, and bop th
? for a Flower. When that's done, get on it and h
the unmarked Block above to get a Coin. Whe
you're finished, enter the Pipe and you'll b
whisked to the end of the level. However, it's n
quite time to leave: if you're Raccoon Mario, fly u
board the Rail Lift in the sky, and collect mo
Coins and a 1-Up before departing 3/1.

3/2: Just go leaping from Ledge to Ledge at th
start, keeping an eye on the water, which will b
rising—or are the Ledges sinking? Fish large an
small will be jumping up at you. When you reac
the long row of Blocks, hit the Jump Block and
Flower will emerge beneath it. The most spectacu
lar way to get to the Flower is to bop the Koopa t
the right and carry its Shell ahead to the dip in th
Ledge. Throw the Shell to the left, smashing th
Blocks so you can get to the Flower. The drawbac
to this tactic is that it'll smash a Switch Block—th
second Block from the right in the same line as th
Jump Block. So, obviously, you'd be wiser to h
the Jump Block, activate the Switch Block, an
then methodically collect the Coins and power-u
Continue to the right, using the Rotary Lift ahe
by jumping on the green fulcrum when the Li

stops spinning. On the Ledge beyond, the top Block will give you a Flower; the one to the left is a Switch Block. (If you don't have Raccoon power, simply pick up a Block on the right and throw it at the Switch Block. By the way—these Blocks can also be used to fight the fish!) There's not much else you need to know about this level. Until you reach the Pipe, the only obstacles hereafter are the rising and falling islands and the leaping fish. When you reach the Pipe, go past it and you'll get a 1-Up Mushroom from the lone glowing Block. Return to the Pipe, enter, and say good-bye to the sea!

World Three Fortress: you'll experience an unhappy sense of déjà vu here! In just one short corridor you have to deal with some old nemeses: two Rotodiscs with a Dry Bones between them, a Thwomp, and another Dry Bones. Leap the first Rotodisc when it's at the four o'clock position, land on Dry Bones as you're coming down, then just shuffle past the next disc. It's more of the same as you continue down the hallway. Now, there're two things you can do to warp right to Boom Boom. First, you can enter the third door in the corridor and quickly press up; this will whisk you right to the Boom Boom room. Or you can enter the *sixth* door. When you go through, head up to the left and enter the first door you come to. This, too, will take you right to Boom Boom. Of course, if you're daring and go to the very end of the corridor, you'll be rewarded with a Coin room. When you enter, make sure you uncover the Invisible Block right over the doorway, or else you won't be able to collect all the riches!

Also, if you're powered-down, you can replenish yourself by going in the *second* door. You'll fall into a sewer; swim to the left and get the power-up in the ? there, then swim to the right and get the next power-up in another ? You're now Raccoon Mario (Swim all the way to the right and, to the left of the last door, you'll notice a Block with a 1-Up. To get to this, try the doors back in the corridor!) You can exit the sewer via the downward-opening Pipe—which will take you back to the main corridor, right under the first Thwomp—or you can go to the steps midway between the two ? Blocks, enter the door at the *top* of the staircase—not the one on the bottom—and you'll be in Boom Boom's room. When you face the boss, you'll have to suppress a yawn: three quick bops and he's chopped liver.

3/4: Wimpy Goombas start things off here, along with Venus Fire Traps in a pair of Pipes. Hug the side of the Pipe until the plants stop firing, then proceed. The ? to the right of the second Pipe is a power-up. Slide down the hill and cut down the Goombas there, then land in the water; jump up on the right side, just above the waterline, and you'll reveal an Invisible Block with a Coin. Get on top of it and jump to the upper left to reveal a second Invisible Block and Coin, then go to the cliff on the right. Mow down the Koopas on the Hill, then bop the ?'s on the other side for Coins. When you reach the downward-facing Pipe, a not-sorely-missed enemy from another game returns: the Lakitu, dropping Spinys on you. Stay on the Ledge of glowing

Blocks and jump on top of the annoying creature when you can. Or there's something else you can do: get a slew of 1-Ups. Remember those Koopas you chopped down a moment ago? When you do that, take the Shell of one of them and go to the two-? Ledge beneath the Pipe—killing the plant within, if you have fireball power. When Lakitu arrives, toss the Shell down so that it shuttles back and forth between the two Blocks on the ground. The Spinys will land in the Shell's path: each time the Shell hits one, you'll get an extra Mario. When you've had your fill, get a Flower from the ? to the right of the Pipe, then activate the Switch Block on the right side of the Ledge below the Pipe. A new Lakitu will arrive in a moment, and you have a few options here. You can get on the next Ledge of ?'s—there's a Coin in the left ?, a power-up in the right—and jump on your foe, or you can race ahead to the end of the round: there's nothing in your way and, though the flying nightmare will flit ahead of you, you'll easily reach the Card before any Spinys are dropped. Lakitu perishes when you get the Card.

3/5: Jelectros try to sizzle you in the sea realm that follows. Since they can't be harmed, give them a wide berth! Moreover, if you have a Frog suit, it's suggested that you use it here! First, if you're Raccoon Mario, stay on top of the water and mount the island to the right. You'll find ten Coins on top. Dive off the island to the left, and go down to the left to get the Coins. Head right, under the L-shaped Ledge: the leftmost of the three ?'s will give you a

Flower, the others will spit out Coins. Make su[re]
you also tap the Blocks to the right of the ? Bloc[k]
for Coins. As you perform all this derring-do, ma[ke]
sure you keep an out out for the Cheep-Cheep[s]
which will be swimming your way. Head rig[ht]
along the bottom of the screen for Coins, then [go]
straight down when you reach the downward-facin[g]
Pipe: there are more Coins to be had. Swim und[er]
the Ledge with the six sea rocks stacked like a rig[ht]
triangle, and, if you're wearing the Frog Suit, y[ou]
can get into the Pipe; if not, forget it. Inside, you['ll]
be rewarded with Coins *and* 1-Ups. If you could[n't]
get in, continue right, hit the row of three ?'s—the[re]
are Coins left and right, and a power-up in the ce[n-]
ter—then go up and over the two Walls. You're [at]
a long downward-facing Pipe: hit up under [it,]
slightly to the right, to uncover an Invisible Blo[ck]
with a 1-Up Mushroom. Continue past the scho[ol]
of sea life and under the island; when you clear t[he]
land mass, swim to the upper right and the surfa[ce.]
Jump up to the island—which should be on yo[ur]
left—and collect the ten Coins on top. Dive back [in]
on the right side, go straight down for the Coi[n]
atop the squat wall, then swim to the right. Wh[en]
you reach the horizontal Pipe, enter . . . and exit [.]

3/6: Time for another Lift level. Get on and off t[he]
Donut Lifts in a hurry, though not so fast that y[ou]
fail to get the power-up from the first ?. Hit t[he]
Block from below, get on the solid Log Ledge to t[he]
right, then collect your reward. Cross the Rota[ry]
Lift to the Donut Lift beyond, and watch out for t[he]

Koopa marching along the Ledge on the right. Kick the creature so that its Shell goes to the right: it'll fall and gather the ten Coins located below. At the end of the next Ledge, jump off onto the back of the flying Koopa and hop left to get onto the Ledge below: the Block there has a power-up. Break the Block overhead to get back to the upper Ledge and hop from Ledge to Ledge. When you come to the two parallel Ledges, get on the lower Ledge, take one of the Blocks and throw it to the right. It'll trigger a Switch Block. Also make sure you jump up and unleash the 1-Up Mushroom, directly overhead; hit the Block on the left side so the Mushroom will roll to the right, allowing you to nab it when it drops through the Coins. Head right to the Rotary Lift and the Exit Pipe.

3/7: The welcoming committee on this level consists of Spike, a little green punk who throws Spiked Balls at you. Though the Balls are deadly, all you have to do is avoid them and bash Spike as you would a Koopa. (Regular Mario doesn't have to do a thing to avoid them: they pass right over his head.) When you begin, get on the Wall and hit the ? for a Coin, then hit the Wall itself for a power-up. Head right. The block of Blocks overhead contains a 1-Up, after which there's nothing much doing until you pass the Pipe. The Block on the ground contains a Flower. Climb the green Hill and get onto the *lower* Ledge to its right. Jump up beneath the *left* side of the Ledge overhead and a Vine will sprout. Climb it to the Coins

in the sky. If you go all the way to the left, you
find a Switch Block that will turn the block
Blocks back on the ground into Coins. When ye
leap back down (off the right), don't go all the wa
to the ground. Rather, land on the Clouds, hop on
the Jump Block and vault to a second Coin heave
Back on the ground, at the end of the level, tl
second Block on the blue staircase contains
power-up.

World Three Fortress: ah . . . more water. Not
ing much to say about this place except that tl
only ? contains a power-up, and there are swarn
of Cheep-Cheeps to deal with. In the first chambe
stay at the top and you'll be able to slip past tl
two Rotodiscs; in the next room, just go where tl
Stretches aren't. At the end, you'll face a spik
Boom Boom, easily beaten when its quills are wit
drawn.

3/8: You'll have a Vine time on this level, b
whatever you do, make sure you get 44 Coins
you can get to the White Mushroom House. H
the first Block you encounter—with your Racco
tail or, if you don't have one, with a Koopa or a
other Block—and a Vine will grow. Use it as
perch to escape the floodwaters. (Don't miss tl
Jump Block while you're up there: it'll give you
power-up.) You'll get the multiple Coins from tl
top Block on the stack of Blocks farther on, ai
a 1-Up from the Block under the Coins—use
Koopa to access it. The next Block contains a
other Vine, as does the next *single* Block aft

that—there's a two-Block slab between them. When you reach the rising and falling Log, use it to go to the lower level of the next plateau. Hit the exposed Switch Block and collect the Coins to the right and above, along with the 1-Up above. If you are the patient type, there's something else you can do here: before hitting the Switch Block, boot a Koopa Shell so that it bops between the Switch Block and the step to the right. Give it a little time, and the Shell will nail the big Boss Bass that comes up at you.

3/9: Eluding the Hanging Piranha Plant that comes charging from the first Pipe, watch out for the Bullet Bills and Bob-Ombs ahead. The fifth Block from the left of the overhead Ledge contains a power-up. The Ledge of ?'s ahead all have Coins. However, that's not what's important here: what matters are unlimited 1-Ups. Instead of killing the Koopa Paratroopa that comes at you at the very start of the level, grab its shell and, when you reach the second Cannon, throw the Shell down so it ricochets between it and the third Cannon—while you, looking to save your overalled self, hop onto the Ledge above the second Cannon . . . that is, the Ledge under the row of ?'s. The Shell will smack against Bullet Bills over and over, earning you points and then 1-Ups. You can also execute this maneuver by getting on top of the Pipe under the second Ledge of ?'s, allowing the Shell to rebound between the third Cannon and the Pipe. Don't go into the Pipe, but continue to the right. When you reach the

Ledge of Jump Blocks, use Blocks from its supp‐
walls to kill Bob-Ombs, then get a power-up fr‐
the leftmost Jump Block. Use a Bob-Omb to ba
through the next wall to the right, then jump
against the leftmost breakable Block for a 1-U
Bust your way through the next set of Blocks to
Pipe beyond. Descend, carrying a Koopa Shell o‐
Block, if one's handy. You can use these agai‐
your foes in the underwater realm. Otherwise,
you need to know about the wet world is that if y
feel like taking a *loooong* swim, there's a Frog S‐
in the Pipe at the left end of this chamber. Incide‐
tally, there's a way to turn Mario invisible in t‐
round—just for fun. (Certainly there's no strate‐
value in having a Mario even you can't see!) Bre‐
down the Block Wall just after the second Cann‐
then squat on the white Wall—the one before
second Cannon—until you fall through. When y
touch down, hurry ahead to the Pipe: if it still lo‐
as though you're in the background as you desce‐
you'll turn transparent. Like we said . . . it's w
derfully pointless!

World Three Ship: some new nemeses here
Rocket Engines and reg'lar ol' Cannonballs.
latter are actually quite useful, since you can ju
from one to the other as you travel. There are a
of Rocky Wrenches here, so you may be hitchin‐
ride on a lot of Cannonballs! When you face Wendy
Koopa, wait until she throws her first Candy Ri‐
then jump on her head and hop to the right. Wh
she rises, slip underneath her to the left. Wait u‐
she throws the next Ring, and repeat. Do this

more time, and she's headed for that great candy shop in the sky.

iant Land

4/1: The giant world is fun. It's no more dangerous than previous worlds, and the oversized props are fun to look at, especially the big, lumbering Goombas. Getting under way: the first ? has a Coin, the second has a power-up. Destroy all the enemies in your way, then fly up to the top of the Pipe Waterfall. In the world above, enter the Pipe on the far left to access a super-secret bonus world where there are a pair of 1-Ups. Back on the ground, get a power-up from the next ? and a Coin from the Block beneath it. On the two-Block Ledge after the Clouds, hop right onto a Koopa and keep hitting successive Koopas without touching the Ledge. You'll earn 1-Ups as before.

4/2: The Pipes sink and rise in the water, but you've had experience with that and should get through with no sweat. When you come to the fifth Pipe—the one with the Blocks on it—use one to demolish the plant in the Pipe to your left, and throw another to the right to liberate the power-up from the ? Block. There's a Starman in the next ? (on the Ledge, just to the right of the exposed Switch Block). Make sure you activate the Switch Block, as collecting 22 Coins in this realm will enable you to get to the White House.

4/3: The Hammer Brothers will attack, one at
time, presenting little challenge: immediately a
ter one jumps up and throws its Hammer, leap
and bash him. Enter the Pipe and you'll be in
world of darkness. It's an easy-to-clear place wi
Buzzies and their friends; nothing you can't ha
dle. There are Coins in the first row of ?'s, and
power-up in the lone Block after the next Ledg
After you get this, start flying up to the right
you can reach the high Ledge which is cover
with Coins. Dropping down the narrow chute
the right side, you'll land on a short slope. Kill t
first Buzzy and kick it into the one on the rigl
Then get on top of the Ledge above and bop t
Ledge over that one to release a 1-Up. Just
careful when you chase it to the right: Spiny
clinging to the ceiling up ahead, prepared
pounce. There's nothing to obtain beyond t
point except Coins.

World Four Fortress: you'll be busy dodging
erything from Hot Foot to Dry Bones, but there a
three important things to remember. First, wh
you come to the Pipes, the third one from the l
is the one you should enter to reach the und
ground chamber. Second, after entering that cha
ber, you'll find a power-up in the second ? from t
right. Third, leave the chamber by uncovering t
two Invisible Blocks in the vertical corridor
the end. Make sure, as you cause them to mate
alize, that you face Boo Diddly: that will tone do
his aggressive tendencies.

4/4: Even if you don't have a Frog Suit, you can reap a good deal in this new water realm. As soon as you hit the churning waters, stand on the Ledge with the ?, get the power-up, and face left. Swim down slowly, making your way to the leftmost Pipe, and enter. It'll take some practice and skill to do this against the current, but it *can* be done. Inside, you'll find two rooms filled with Coins—well . . . they'll be filled with Coins after you trigger the Switch Blocks. When you emerge you'll be attacked by a Lakitu; the danger here is that the current might carry you right smack into a Spiny. There's nothing else to worry about in this realm.

4/5: Grabbing a Koopa, use it to smash the right side of the Pyramid; the ? has a power-up. After the Pipe, you'll face three Cannons in succession, each one higher than the one before it; as a result, Bullet Bills are plentiful. After the first Cannon, hit the middle ? of the Ledge above to get a power-up. The rest of the ?'s, and the ones in the next Ledge, are all Coins. You'll pass a Cloud with Coins over it, then a pair of Pipes and a clutch of Cannons; you're going to have to hop on top of a Bullet Bill in order to reach the lone Block overhead: bumping up against that Block will release a Vine, which will take you to a sky chamber. There, get the Tanooki Suit, activate the Switch Block, and collect the Coins that trail off into the skies. More Cannons and the Exit Pipe await on the ground.

4/6: Two important things in the first square of

Blocks overhead: a Starman and 1-Up. After y
get past the killer Plant in the first Pipe, you ha
the option of entering the doorway beyond; do s
and every foe in the giant world will becom
normal-sized. The next ? has a power-up, and if y
opted to change everything to normal size, and y
fly into the sky here, you'll get Coins and a 1-U
among the Clouds. On the ground there's a Sta
man in the second Block up of the Wall supporti
the Ledge; the Ledge itself will give you multip
Coins. Jump up between the next two Pipes: the
are three Invisible Blocks here, all of them contai
ing Coins. However, if you changed everything fr
giant to small, one Block will give you a 1-Up. T
next door you encounter, like the first, will chan
the size of everything in this realm.

World Four Fortress: this is the toughest a
most exciting fortress you've encountered thusfa
The first chamber is similar to others in whi
you've faced Dry Bones and had to cross Don
Lifts. Get the power-up from the only ? here, a
don't stand on the Lifts too long: remember, they
fall if you do. Now, when you reach the bend in t
corridor—a reverse L—you'll find a Block. It's
Switch Block: activate it, and a rectangle fram
by Coins will appear to the left. Step into the re
tangle, press up on the controller, and you'll ent
an Invisible Doorway. Hop on the Arrow Lift a
head up—the Lifts move in whatever direction t
Arrow is pointing—but make sure you don't hit yo
head on something while on this or *any* Lift. Do
and the Lift'll disappear. (*Why* is there a chan

that you'll bump your head? Because, fellow Mario-
ites, you have to jump on some of the Lifts to get
the Arrows to change direction.) This room is a vertical chamber, and you have to navigate your way
through a maze of Pipes. Go up, right, switch Lifts
and go up, hop to get the Lift to go left, go up, then
get off the Lift and hop over the Pipe with the Piranha Plant to the downward-facing Pipe beyond. Enter, get the power-up from the ? above, go through
the opening in the Pipes above, pass through the
opening in the upper left, enter the break in the
Ledge on the upper right, and exit via the Pipe. (If
you're a little more adventurous, explore the Pipes
here: never know when you might find secret rooms
with Invisible Blocks, Coins, and 1-Ups!) Back in
the main corridor, watch out for the Rotodisc as you
advance, then brain Boom Boom three times as before.

World Four Ship: the last ship introduced the Bolt
Lift, an optional, corkscrewing Elevator that will
carry you safely through rough spots. It's here, too,
and more useful than before; when you encounter
it—over the Rocket Engines—jump on and keep
hopping to move it ahead. To the right of the Bolt
Lift is a ? with a power-up; another ?/power-up is
located to the right of the Pipe at the end of the
ship. Overall, this is actually a pretty simple level.
All of the Cannons here are Rocket Engines, and
as long as you proceed slowly, dashing ahead when
each Rocket shuts down, you'll be okay. Watch out
for the occasional Rocky Wrench. As for Iggy

Koopa—he's dogmeat if you hit him three tim‹
outside of his Shell.

Sky Land

5/1: If you've gotten this far—more than halfway
you don't need a blow-by-blow guide to the gam‹
Hereafter, we'll give you the high points. In th‹
realm, fly up and slightly to the right to enter t‹
Sky Pipe. Inside, there are two ways to go: squ‹
and leap and you'll enter a tight corridor that lea‹
to a Jump Block and the end of the realm. *Don't ‹*
that way. Take the lower route and you'll reach ‹
island where there are four 1-Ups. Don't forget
fly skyward, activate the Switch Block, collect t‹
Coins, then bust your way out.

5/2: As you drop, use your tail—if you've got on‹
obviously—to brake your descent. Hit the Jun
Blocks to get up to the Pipe—otherwise, you've g
a long and dangerous journey ahead of you, wi
very few rewards. If you got up to the Pipe, ent‹
the next Pipe you encounter to access a room whe‹
there are three 1-Ups.

5/3: This realm plays from right to left. Hiding ju
beyond the second Pipe is a Goomba wearing t‹
poundiferous Kuribo's Shoe. Lure the Goomba bac‹
to the Ledge on the right, then jump up against t‹
Block on which it comes to rest. You'll get the Sh‹

and with it you can crush any foe. Even without it, there are no big surprises here.

World Five Fortress: break the first overhead Ledge and fly up. Head up and right to the Pipe. Enter, and follow the Arrow to fly up and uncover three Invisible Blocks containing 1-Ups. Thwomps and Rotodiscs are the foes here.

World Five Tower: more Thwomps and Rotos. When you reach the sky, the right block on each Tower is a Pile Driver Micro Goomba. After reentering the Tower and reemerging in the sky, get onto the Clouds under the four-Block Ledge. Hit the second Block from the left to activate a Vine, and climb to the next realm.

5/4: Fly up after the second Rotary Lift, so you can collect the Coins there. Don't get swallowed by the Waterfalls down below. Again, land on the fulcrum of each Rotary Lift for the most stable footing.

5/5: Kick away the Blocks on the second Pipe and enter for Coins and a Tanooki Suit. You'll be deposited near the end; there are power-ups in the top right Block of the overhead structure, and in the Block just beyond it, on the ground. If you didn't enter the Pipe, you can get the Coins below the Donut Lifts by standing on each Lift in turn, letting it drop, and collecting the Coin as it falls—making sure you jump off before it vanishes.

5/6: Jump onto Para-Beetles' backs to cross this realm. The only ? has a power-up.

5/7: Don't rush into this world: get a Starman the Map. If you do so, you can obtain Starmen peatedly to get you through the realm. You'll fi them in the first, fourth, seventh, and eighth ? the low Block on the other side of the next Wa and the Block over the Pipe. If you enter the fir Pipe, you'll find yourself in a world rich with goo ies. Use a P-Wing to go to the top of the screen an hit the Switch Block; it's tough to do as plain o Raccoon Mario. Also, squat on the White Wall the end until you drop through it. When you ex via the Pipe above, you'll have extended invincib ity. Beware Micros on this level.

World Five Fortress: a Starman in the rightmo Block of the first Ledge of ?'s will help you. Racco Mario can fly through here, no trouble.

5/8: There's a power-up in the third ? from the le in the overhead Ledge. Get it: you'll need it to su vive the Lakitu onslaught. The wisest tack here to race—and we mean *race*—ahead rather than t to fight the rat: vantage points from which to jun down are much too few. You should take no mo than 20 seconds to get through here. When you g to the Card section, wait: when Lakitu has tosse a quartet of Spinys, jump up and get the Car You'll be rewarded with points *and* a 1-Up.

5/9: Fire Chomps chase you as you hop fro vertically-moving Elevator to Elevator. If you' Raccoon Mario, fly above the Elevators, alighti only when necessary. This will give you the mobility you'll need to bop the Chomps.

World Five Ship: heavier artillery than usual here makes for a difficult passage. You'll certainly have to hop on Cannonballs and Bullet Bills to get through it. The boss here, Roy, doesn't jump in patterns like his fellow fiends, so you'll have to watch him. Keep your distance and leap only when he gives you an opening.

Land

6/1: Ptooies make their debut here, but you can vault their Spiked Balls with ease. After the first Pipe, fly up to the doorway overhead. Enter, shimmy under the big Blocks, and hit the Switch Block. If you start this level with a Starman, you'll find another in the ? before the floating Coins.

6/2: The Clouds on this level shuttle back and forth like Elevators. Be careful not to get yourself trapped on the left side of a Ledge or Wall, especially when the screen begins moving upward, or you'll be scrolled off the screen.

World Six Fortress: stay on the Elevator here, or you'll never get across the Spikes. Watch out for the Rotodiscs during the vertical section of your Elevator trip. You can jump down this passage if you want, poising on the overhanging Wall and waiting until the Disc goes down. Enter the door at the end

of the ride; reenter as often as you wish to re-
quire the power-up in the ? Block.

6/3: You can run across gaps in the Columns
holding down the B button. On the L-shaped Ledg
hurl a Koopa at the floating Block ahead to activa
a Vine. Climb and enter the Pipe.

6/4: The lone Block by the big Ice Wall has a 1-U
hit the Block on the right so the Mushroom go
left, or you'll lose it. On the Elevator: as soon as
passes below the small Ice Wall, jump up to reve
an Invisible Jumping Block. Hop on for a trip to
Coin bank in the sky! Back on the ground, to t
left of the icy runway is a Wall with a Switch Bloc
Activate it and run right—sliding *under* the Rota
Lift. Fly up to get to the 1-Up in the air.

6/5: Fly up after the ? to get to a Ledge with
1-Up. Back on the ground, bust down all the Bloc
on the straightaway *after* the slope, kill a Koop
and fly up. At the right side of the Wall up abov
toss the Shell against the Nipper Plants to destr
them. Enter the Pipe to leave. If you want a litt
more danger, don't fly up yet but continue rig
The horizontal Pipe at the very end leads to
power-up room which you can exit and reenter
often as you wish.

6/6: Go down and get the Starman from the t
Block on the rightmost of the two Walls. Bewa
the Cheep-Cheeps leaping from the Pools beyo

In the water section, swim at once to the upper right for a 1-Up, then swim back down—this area is a dead end.

World Six Fortress: the Thwomps move from side to side here. They're easy to elude if you move cautiously. Boom Boom's pretty lethargic, making him easy to beat. The only ? here is a power-up.

6/7: The big challenge is negotiating all the Donut Lifts. Otherwise, there's not too much going on here. If you gather 78 Coins, the White Mushroom House will put in an appearance, so make that a goal. Only Fiery Mario can thaw the Coins at the end of the level.

6/8: Neat trick time: catch a Koopa right away, knock the Shell to the right, and run after it, pressing the B button. My, how the Nipper Plants will fall! When you come to the Ice Blocks later on, make sure you carry one to the Hill beyond to knock out more 'noying Nippers. Upon reaching the Switch Block, activate it, then use a P-Wing to fly up quickly and collect the 88 Coins in the sky. Incidentally, there's a totally useless trick you can do at the end of this level: there's a tunnel just before the Switch Block; enter with the P-Wing, and you can flutter underground to the left.

6/9: Go down the Pipe—there's nothing to the right worth getting. Swimming right, you can enter the first Pipe only if you're wearing a Frog Suit; inside are 35 Coins and a trio of 1-Ups. When you exit,

swim up. Fly around the right side of the fat W
above until you find a Switch Block. Activate
and all the Munchers below will turn to Coins. F
this realm via the last Pipe on the *top*.

6/10: After the second Pipe, cross the Ledge to
right and drop to the Blocks beyond it. Dest
Buster Beetle, then hit the Block on the right w
an Ice Block and a Vine will sprout. Click on
Switch Block (far left) and the big batch of Blo
to the right will turn into a colossal collectior
Coins. Fiery Mario can liberate tons of Coins b
on the ground . . . but, more important, he can th
the ice over a Pipe and get the Hammer Broth
Suit located inside. (This suit is not only usefu
the fortress, but, if you squat while wearing it,
Piranha Plants can't harm you!)

World Six Fortress: either fly through this on
your Raccoon Suit or don the Hammer Suit so
can destroy Thwomps and Boo Diddlies. Speak
of Boo Diddly, if you face away from the creat
it will attack . . . at which point you can spin s
denly and leap over it. When you cross the C
veyor Belt near Thwomp, unless you pelt
blockhead with Hammers, it'll be necessary to ju
up and down—thus preventing yourself from m
ing ahead—until the big lunk moves. While yo
doing this, be sure not to back into the Rotodisc
the final room, pelt the Boo Diddlies with Hamm
or simply evade them as the floor rises, bring
you to the door.

World Six Ship: take the high route so you

collect the power-ups. You've been in spots like this before. As for Lemmy Koopa, get him between tosses of his Circus Balls.

e Land

7/1: A big, busy vertical realm of Pipes is your introduction to this world, but apart from learning which one leads where, you won't have much trouble here. Get a power-up from the ? to the right of the Jump Block by killing a Koopa and tossing its Shell to the right of the ?. It'll ricochet back into the ?. Below the Pipe you're on there's an Invisible Block with a 1-Up, should you need it. Slightly above this section is a narrow Pipe, broken in the center. If you're Raccoon Mario, get rid of the Koopa—ditch it through the gap in the Pipes—go right, then run to the left, flying up to the Pipe below the Coin room. Enter to collect the riches.

7/2: Use a Frog Suit here. Descend via the second Pipe and swim left. Collect the Coins, then hit the Switch Block—don't do it the other way around! Swim hurriedly to the right to get the Coins before they revert to being Blocks. Exit via the last Pipe on the right, and jump up to uncover all the Jump Blocks. (Yes, we know you've covered your overhead exit. Never fear!) Go down the Pipe to the right, get the power-up on the left, go back up the Pipe, reenter the Pipe on the left, swim left, leave the water, and move overground, now, to the right.

Cross the bridge of Jump Blocks. (If it weren't he
you couldn't get over!) Enter the Pipe after
Jump Blocks, clear out the goodies down here, e
and leave the level using the fourth Block from
right at the end.

7/3: You can Starman your way through this le
Hit the first ? for a Starman, run using B butto
the next Starman ? (leftmost of the four you'll
counter), rush ahead to the next identical setup
another Starman, and get the next one in the ?
ter the Pipe. There are two more Starmen in b
Blocks on either side of the vertical Pipe. At
end of the level, use the B button to run right acr
the Pits ... including the humongous one at
end. Note: if you instinctively activate the Swi
Block, you end your chances of getting all the St
men. Also, if you hit a Starman Block when you
not invincible, all you'll get is Coins.

7/4: Before entering the Pipe to start, fly over
Wall for a pair of 1-Ups. Otherwise, this level
more of the familiar hijinks underwater. The
section that'll test your mettle is the Blooper f
with Big Bertha roaming through it. You'll have
negotiate this dense region with quick, little mo
ments.

7/5: When you go down the first Pipe after
Ledge, grab the Bob-Omb waiting down there a
hurl it against the others coming from the rig
That'll give you some breathing time. The intere

ing and challenging thing about this realm is the number of Invisible Blocks you encounter. Jump up in virtually any gap and you'll find one; it's fun but, obviously, you don't want to box yourself into an area. Before you bop, make sure there's a back door! At the end of the level, you have to uncover all of the Invisible Blocks to build a bridge by the L-shaped Ledge. Otherwise, you can only get out if you're Raccoon Mario.

Piranha Garden: Piranha Plants infest this level. There are two sections. In the first, cross the Pipes by taking small hops from Pipe to Pipe, moving to each new one as the Plant there is going down. (Some players prefer big, fat B button leaps . . . but those are a little reckless compared to little steps which allow you to plan each one.) In either case, a misstep and Mario is Plant food! In the next section of Pipes 'n' Piranha Plants, the first Jump Block contains a Starman. When you reach the three Pipes at the end, take the one in the middle to get out.

World Seven Fortress: first, go up on the silvery-blue Ledge, go right, and uncover the Switch Block. That'll turn every Block in this library of Blocks into a Coin. When you're done, take the door on the Ledge, go right and down the Pipe, claim the Tanooki Suit, and enter the horizontal Pipe at the end. Collect the bonuses in this room. Exit using the door at the bottom left, and reenter as often as you wish to replenish your power-ups. When you're through, leave via this bottom left door and head

left. Go past the door and fly up. Enter the Pipe
the ceiling to battle the Boomster.

7/6: This one's fun . . . but frustrating when you
first getting to know the ropes. First, it's full
those multidirectional Lifts identical to those in
World Four Fortress—the ones you jump on
change direction. Only not all of them change wh
you leap. A few key strategies: the second Lift yo
use passes some Spike-covered Ledges. To get
the two Ledges, switch sides on the Lift as it pass
the Ledge. You can—and should!—pass through t
first vertical Pipe you encounter flush against t
right wall. When you ride your Lift past the
ranha Plants in the Pipes on top, simply shift
the opposite side of the Lift to escape the car
vores' teeth.

7/7: If you're not Raccoon Mario, you can get acr
the sea of Munchers here by using Starmen. The
are four ? Blocks, each with a Starman: liberate t
pointy helpers as you pass the Block and run aft
the Starman . . . but *don't* catch it until your pr
ent dose of invincibility is about to wear out. O
erwise, you won't have enough Starman power
get you all the way to the end.

7/8: Fireballs are *really* useful against the Piran
Plants here. If you don't have it, watch your st
There's a Starman in the leftmost ? atop the gr
Wall—after the second downward-facing Pipe. Ju
up along the right side of the third downward-faci

Pipe—the one over the white Wall—to reveal an Invisible Jump Block. Get on it to vault to a celestial bank! Shortly beyond that Block, you'll find three pipes together: a tall one to the right of a pair of squat ones. When the Ptooie retreats, go down the leftmost Pipe to get a Hammer Brothers Suit.

7/9: This one's a maze, and the clock's your real enemy here. Here's the route: go up at the Jump Blocks, up/left through the gap, up/right through the next gap, then left through two Walls and up the gap to the left of the second Wall. Rush along the top, cross the two Ledges, stay on the top until you reach the Jump Blocks, then drop to the left of them, go through the Wall, go up/left through the gap, through the next Wall to the left, down, right, down, right—under the Ledge of ?'s—up/right through the gap, go through two Walls to the right, go up the Ledges, right across the Pipe, through the Wall, down and left through the Wall, down through the gap, right through the Wall, up/right through the gap, then right and down. Enter the Pipe to leave. Stop and hit ?'s *only* if there's time.

World Seven Fortress: this is a museum of menace, with all the worst foes. If you have a Raccoon or Hammer Brothers Suit—wear it. There's a Starman in the first Block—after the third Pipe. Enter the last Pipe on the right—beneath the overhang—to meet the boss.

World Seven Ship: to go from platform to platform here, use Raccoon Mario *or* press the B button

when you jump. Otherwise, the only way to cr
the ship is by using the troublesome Bolt Lifts.

Dark Land

Tanks: you must battle increasingly larger Ta
in this level. One key to surviving is to leap off ea
successive Tank when the tip of the barrel of t
next Tank appears on the right. The second-to-l
Tank has two Cannons for a double attack; get
top of the upper barrel as quickly as possible.

Battleships: there's a 1-Up to be had on the ri
side of the first Mast. Don't jump up to get
though, until the Cannon behind has fired! The
portant, secret strategy to master here is learni
how to swim beneath the Battleships. It's difficu
but it can be done.

Hand Attack: as you cross the Bridges here,
ant hands will shoot up to grab you. They're not
tough to avoid. If you let them grab you, you'll
taken to secret worlds; not bad if you're a skil
player and can fight your way out. The rewards :
worthwhile.

Airships: if you're not Raccoon Mario, have Ha
mers or fireballs to take out the Rocky Wrench
It's best to position yourself on the Rocket Eng
when jumping to the next Airship.

8/1: Fly up; the Switch Block will fill the air be
with Coins. The fifth (super-tall) Pipe contains th
1-Ups.

8/2: Enter the quicksand, enter one of the Pipes, and you'll pop up right near the end of the level.

World Eight Fortress: this is a realm of secret doors which will really power you up! When you reach the Blocks forming a big H, activate the Switch Block on top. Enter the door below it, and you'll access a secret room and a 1-Up. After you're attacked by a trio of Thwomps, go up the Staircase and continue right. After the second window, you'll find a Switch Block; hit it, head left, go in the door, go down and left and into another door. The leftmost of the three Blocks contains a 1-Up. On the bottom level of the Fortress, the door below the Thwomp allows for repeated entry and, thus, multiple power-ups. Toward the end of the lower level, climb the Staircase and continue ahead to two Blocks underfoot. The right Block contains a Switch Block. Hit it for access to the power-up on the upper door.

Super Tank: in general, stay roughly one-quarter screen length from the right, so you can deal *immediately* with what's ahead. Rocky Wrench traffic is heavy here, so be ready to make quick, short moves back or ahead to dodge the homicidal handymen.

Koopa Castle: beware the Statues here—they fire lasers. As you make your way through the maze of the Castle, always take the high path when you have a choice. When you reach Bowser, the tack to take is simple: let him kill himself! Stand on the third Block in from the left, let him jump at you,

and scurry to the same position on the right. [
leap will dig a pit. He'll jump after you at your r
position, digging a new pit; when he leaps, you s
ply run into the first pit he dug. He'll jump a
you; get up and out of the way *fast*, and he'll l
in the pit, digging it deeper. Repeat this proc
over and over until he digs his way through the
layers of Blocks to the bottom of the screen . . . a
death.

AFTERWORD

Hope you enjoyed this trip through all four Mario-lands.

Many of you have written asking about a tip we gave in *How to Win at Nintendo Games* #1, about the mysterious "water world" at the end of 1-2 in *Super Mario Bros.*

Most of you say it doesn't work for you.

Well . . . it doesn't always work for us either! We don't know why, but that's one of the mysteries of Mario, we guess.

While we're on the subject, here's another tip that has worked at the same spot—though, again, not every time: if you face the left side of the screen, jump up and break all of the Blocks on top *except* the one next to the Pipe, you can also reach the wet world by walking through the wall.

Give it a try. Then write, in care of the publisher, to let us know how you make out!

In fact, many readers have written with com-

ments about our previous Nintendo Games boo‍
Though there isn't space to acknowledge all of ‍
correspondents, a few whose letters were parti‍
larly interesting are: Eric Acosta, Tony Basso, ‍
Bowen, Jason Bustard, Charlie Davis, John Detr‍
John Doty, Darren Ebert, Sean Fain, Chris Fe‍
rowicz, Bree Frick, Bo Hakala, Scott Hanlin, D‍
iel Healy, Fayaz Jamal, Chris Katides, Michael‍
Kugelman, Joey Lee, Keith Lock, Jeffrey Lubi‍
James McIntire, Chris Mapes, Eric Medley, ‍
Moorman, Kyle Orwig, Jon Peaslee, Bo Peders‍
James Picou, Kevin Preusse, Brian Richards, Dor‍
Roberts, Jesse Rowlett, Jason Schneider, Da‍
Schoenberger, Tom Schrantz, Jack Small, Greg‍
Alan Smith, Mary K. Spencer, Jim Thompson, ‍
Sarah Whitlock.

Deepest thanks of all to some highly-treasu‍
readers: Jeremy Cate, Alan Fuller, Tony Rizzo, ‍
Walpole, and Laura Wood.

See you all in the next book. Until then, ha‍
videogaming!